Don't Mention the Children

Michael Rosen

Smokestack Books
1 Lake Terrace, Grewelthorpe, Ripon HG4 3BU
e-mail: info@smokestack-books.co.uk
www.smokestack-books.co.uk

ISBN 978-0-9931490-2-3

Smokestack Books is
represented by Inpress Ltd

for Emz

Contents

Introduction

I've written these poems, thoughts, reveries and squibs over the last two or three years. In my mind they clump together into three different types or categories: the political, the autobiographical and the surreal. Yet, given that my politics is of the kind that regards the auto-biographical and the surreal as political, the categories break down at the very moment that I've created them. Perhaps then, this line of thought would be more fruitful, if I mention that I think of these poems as starting out from three different kinds of impulses. So, sometimes it's from wanting to unpick and contradict the ways in which the world is described to us by those in power. Other times it's to investigate the things that happened to me, my parents and their relatives. Other times it's to experiment with the world I meet: as I walk about London, I see what might happen if I shift some of the personnel and circumstances from the real to the unreal.

For many writers, writing is an act of discovery, we ask: what will I discover, if I write like this... or like that? I hope that when I write in that spirit – as I have with this book – it will lead readers to make discoveries too.

Michael Rosen
May 2015

A whale got on my bus

I was on a bus
and a whale got on.
The recorded announcement said:
'Please move down the bus
so that there is room for passengers
getting on the bus.
Please move down the bus
so that there is room for passengers
getting on the bus.'

We moved down the bus
and the whale squeezed in
and the doors closed.

I was next to the whale.
It said, 'Sorry, I'm dripping.'
'No worries,' I said,
'same thing happens to me
when I'm wearing my waterproof coat.'
'What this much?' said the whale.
I didn't want to make the whale feel bad
so I said,
'Well, yes actually.'
'Do people complain?' the whale said.
And I lied,
I said,
'Yes,' when in actual fact no one
had ever complained.
'I can't see all the way round the back of me,'
the whale said, 'could you look to see
if I'm dripping over everyone back there?'
'Sure,' I said and I looked.
People were getting showered.
'There's a bit of dripping going on,' I said.
'I knew it,' said the whale.

'Do you have a towel on you?'
'No,' I said, 'I don't usually carry a towel around.'
'Well,' said the whale, 'isn't that typical!'
'Is it?' I said.
'You get on a bus, you're dripping wet
you ask for a bit of help, a bit of sympathy,
and all you get is nastiness.
What is it with people, these days?'
'I'm sorry,' I said, 'I just don't have a towel.'

And then it all went quiet.
It was all a bit tense.
Awkward.

All you could hear was a
dripping sound.
Drip, drip, drip,drip...

Sign

The sign on the train alarm said: 'Break cover'.
I looked over my shoulder, checked my bag
and headed out into the crowd.
No one spotted me.

So far so good.

Alchemy

I had been on my own in my office for about three
hours. It's on the top floor of a converted factory.
I don't lock the door. People don't drop in. It hasn't
got my name up. So I'm sitting at my table when a
young guy walked in and said, 'Have you got any
books on alchemy?'
'No,' I said, 'I don't think I do.'
He said, 'That's a shame because I've been doing
some alchemy. My brother is a musician but I'm not
going to go down that path.'
I said, 'Alchemy was big a few hundred years ago.'
He said, 'Really? Wow.'
I said, 'People in Shakespeare's time were keen on
it. Actually,' I said, 'what a coincidence, I've got a book
about a man called John Dee, right here. I'll look in the
index. Oh yes,' I said, 'there is lots in here about alchemy.'
'Are all these books yours?' he said.
I said, 'Yes.'
'Can I buy that one off you?'
'No,' I said.
He said, 'What are you doing here?'
I said, 'I'm writing.'
He started laughing.
I said, 'I'll write down the title of the John Dee book.'
'To tell the truth,' he said, 'I don't really do reading.'
'No worries,' I said, 'can you use Google?'
'Yeah, yeah,' he said.
'Well,' I said, 'just google "alchemy" and see where it takes you.'
'Yes,' he said, 'I'll do that.'

Conversation on a bus

Boy: Are you Michael Rosen?
Me: Yes.
Boy: Really?
Me: I am Michael Rosen.
Boy: You look just like him.

Airport

I was in a car to the airport. The couple I was
with had an agreement to help each other get
anxious.
He said, 'It's in the bag I'm taking on board.'
She said, 'It won't go through security.'
He said, 'This is the worst airport in the world.'
'You're doing it again,' she said.
'YOU'RE doing it again,' he said.
The driver jammed on the brakes.
'Bloody hell,' said the husband, 'that woman's
got a death wish. Came straight out.'
'Shush,' said the woman, 'you're not driving.
Drop us off next to the trolleys,' she added.
'Drop us off next to the trolleys,' said the
husband.
'I've told him that,' she said.

The driver drove past the sign:
'Terminal set down'.
'There!' said the husband, 'Terminal set down.'
'I saw it already,' said the driver.

Beards

There's a cafe I go to when I've got time to kill.
I was sitting having a drink and a tomato sandwich
when a guy sat down at my table. He kept
looking at me. I tried to ignore him. Then he said,
'I hate beards.'
I've got a beard. I looked at him. He had a beard.

Dustman

I said to the dustman, 'You're taking my stuff.'
'Yep,' he said.
I said, 'Everything in this bin matters.'
He said, 'C'mon pal, we're on a tight turnaround here,'
I said, 'You're taking my stuff.'
He called to his mates, 'We've got one here.'
I said, 'That's my past you're taking.'
He said, 'Uh-huh.'
I said, 'I haven't got any other past. I can't go out and
buy someone else's past and pretend it's mine. All
the stuff in here happened to me.'
He said, 'Am I taking it or not?'
I said, 'Why are you asking me? This is all much
bigger than a yes-no thing. It's about identity. And
culture.'
'And bins,' he said.
'We are what we throw away,' I said, 'and you're
a cog in a machine that is cutting us down to
size. The machine doesn't want us to know who
we are. And the way it's doing this is to cut us
off from our pasts. It's not your fault,' I said, 'you
have to earn a living, but you've become a tool
in their hands.'
He said, 'I'll just do next door's. If you change your mind
in the meantime, I'll come back and get yours.'

The book

He was in an alleyway between two old factories
and someone had set up a secondhand bookshop
in one of them. The books weren't in any order.
There were piles of books on the floor. He moved
about looking at the titles. He knew that in shops like
this, the books are often in groups. He spotted one
group that looked like a group of books of short stories.
He picked one up. Started reading. As he read it, he
realised that it told the story of his own life: what he
had done, what he was doing, what he thought about,
what he ate, the man his wife was having an affair with.
He bought the book. Took it home. He read on: the wife
of the man in the book asked the man to wait, the man
agreed to wait, it was an arrangement, maybe the affair
would last, maybe it wouldn't, so he waited. He went on
waiting. The End. The man who found the book put it
back on the shelf and left it there. He went home. His
wife said to him that the affair was not coming to an end.
She asked him to wait. She said, I want you to wait. He
said no. She said that he was a bastard. People wait,
she said. He said, yes, he knew that, but he wouldn't.

Hair

I opened up a packet of bread the other day,
took out a slice and as I put the butter on I
noticed that there was a hair in the bread. Not
on the slice. It was in the bread. It wasn't
very long. I didn't fancy eating it, so I put the
slice back in the packet and put the packet
in the bin. In the morning, I was looking around
for something to eat for breakfast, and I didn't
have anything in, so I thought, ah, maybe I
could fish that loaf out of the bin, pull the
slice with the hair in it out of the packet and
maybe eat one of the other slices. So I got
it out the bin, opened up the packet and the slice
that had the hair in was on the top. Now
it had several hairs. I looked closely at it and
I could see that the hair was growing out of the
bread. This wasn't mould. I know what that hairy
mould looks like. This was hair. It was a browny
colour with little blonde touches. I put it back in
the bin and went off to work. When I came back
from work, I got the packet out again and
sure enough, it had grown more hair. Now there
was enough hair to make it look like it was the top
of someone's head. All growing out of one slice.
It even had a parting. Then, without knowing
why, I picked up this slice with the hair on it
and started to eat it. I was right about the hair.
It was hair. The bread had changed though. It
didn't really taste like bread. More like something
made out of walnut. I ate it and pulled the hair out
of my mouth. It wasn't really hairy. More furry than
hairy.

Dentist

I had to go to the dentist a few weeks ago. It was for a crown. The dentist explained to me that it's like a false tooth that sits on the wreck of your own tooth. Fine by me. I went in one day for the 'prep' and then a fortnight later for the crown. The dentist said that it would take quite a time. When I'm at the dentist I shut my eyes and do stretches with my shoulders and neck. I go into a trance. I hear the dentist and his assistant as if they are at the other end of a corridor. I heard, 'That's it.' I got up, said thanks and walked out. For a few days I didn't think to look in my mouth to see the crown. I leaned into the mirror and could just make out a tiny clock face. The dentist had fixed it, face up in the tooth, the tooth being on the bottom row. I rushed back to the dentist, went up to the receptionist and asked to see him. The receptionist said that he had left. He wasn't working at this dentist's any more.
I said, 'Look! He's put a tiny clock in there.'
I opened my mouth. She looked in and said, 'It says twenty past five. That's the right time.'

Car alarm

I wondered if car alarms go off in the night
because they feel unappreciated. When they
go off, do they know that people have turned over
in their beds thinking about them? The other night,
an alarm was going off in bursts of eighteen.
Then a pause. Then another eighteen. After
about five bursts, I tried counting in between.
It came out as twelve. After the tenth burst the
alarm changed. A second beat came in, then a
guitar. It was a remix of that song they released
after Bob Marley died, 'Blackman Redemption'. In
fact, I think the release was a remix... I went
downstairs and put on a pair of trousers. I went
into the street, walked down to the car and I was
right. I wondered whether there was any recording
of Bob Marley doing it without the remix. After that
bit where it goes, 'Spread ou-ou-ou-out...', it went
back to doing the alarm. Bursts of eighteen. I
counted the twelve in between and went back
indoors to bed.

Walking

I was knocked over in the road near our house
and was in hospital for several months. When
they thought I was well enough, they said that
I should try to walk. They took me to the door
of the ward and said, 'Walk down the corridor.'
I looked ahead. There were double doors and
beyond that more double doors and beyond that
more double doors and more beyond that.
I thought of other corridors... all corridors.
They said, 'Just think of one step at a time.'
I had forgotten how to walk. I put one foot
forward. The other foot wouldn't move very far.
It was OK about coming up alongside the first
foot. But it wouldn't go on. It stopped right there.
Alongside the first foot.
'Put one hand on the wall, if you want.'
I looked ahead to the double doors. I could get
there, I thought, so long as I don't try anything
clever. Don't try that thing where you put one
foot forward and swing the other foot past the
first foot. So I did one foot forward, bring the
other foot up to join it. One foot forward, bring
the other foot up to join it. I looked ahead. There
was no end to this corridor.

Cows

We went for a walk
and we went past a farm
and on towards some woods
and past the woods
out to an empty sort of a place
and no one lived there
but there was a tower
and we walked up to the tower
and it was full of cows,
I figured that the cows
had run away from the farm
and were living in the tower.
It was a cow tower.
I was trying to work out
how the cows got to the top
of the tower when I saw
some doors open
and a cow walked out.
It was a lift,
the cows were using the lift,
and my dad said,
'Phew, there's a bit of pong,
isn't there?'
And I said, 'That cow's pressing
the wrong button.
It's pressing the button
that keeps the doors open.
It'll never go.'
My Dad said,
'Good point, Mick.'

The whooshing sound

The doctor asked me to sit still
and then he handed me
a thing that looked a bit like a plug
and asked me to put it over my bellybutton.

I did that.

Then he attached a tube to the plug
and switched on a machine.

There was a whooshing sound.

For a while nothing happened
but then I started to feel my belly
swelling up.

'You'll feel your belly swelling up,'
the doctor said.

'Yes,' I said.

It felt a bit like having a tight belt on,
or maybe having a bit too much to eat.

'It may feel a bit like having a tight belt on,
or having a bit too much too eat,' he said.

'Yes,' I said.

I went on swelling up
and I started to feel light,
as if I wasn't sitting so heavily in the chair.

The machine went on making the whooshing sound.

Then, very slowly, very gently,
I found myself lifting off the chair.

'Were you expecting this to happen?'
I said.
'Yes and no,' the doctor said.
'What happens when it's a no?'
I said.
'Oh... sometimes, it leaks,'
he said,
'I'm in the air,' I said.
'Yes,' he said.

I was floating round the room.
'Oh,' he said, 'did I weigh you?'
'No,' I said.
'It's a bit late now,' he said.
'Yes,' I said, 'I wouldn't know how to come down
from up here and stand on the scales.'
'What's your date of birth?' he said.

The window was open.
I looked out.
I don't know if it was because I looked,
or if it was because of the way the wind
was blowing
but I found myself drifting towards the window.

'I think I'm floating out of the window,'
I said.
'What did you say was your date of birth?'
he said.
'I am floating out of the window,'
I said.
'Is it, the 4th of June 19..?
I didn't catch the rest
I was out the window and
too far off.
Too far away.

Cucumber

There was a cucumber in the lost property office.
It was found near the ticket barrier at the station.
No one came in to say it was theirs. The cucumber
sat on the shelf. It started to go soft. But still no
one came. Then it started to flatten out and go
mushy. The skin stayed more or less the same.
A bit wrinkly but still like a cucumber skin. Inside
the cucumber became goo. It was smelling quite
strong. A fruity earthy smell. After a bit more time,
it started going dark grey. And fruit flies flew around it.
Then, about six months after the cucumber was
put in the lost property office, a man came in and
said, 'Have you got a cucumber?'
The lost property office assistant said, 'I'll have
a look in the book.'
He got the book out and it said, 'Cucumber.'
'Can I ask you where you think you lost the
cucumber?' he said.
The man said, 'No, I'm sorry. I got on the train,
got off the train and went home. When I got home
I looked in my bag and the cucumber was gone.'
'Can you tell me which station you got on at, and
which station you got off at?'
'Well, my problem is that I got on and off at quite
a few stations that day,' said the man, 'and I can't
remember them all. You see I deliver stuff for
people.'
'Do you deliver cucumbers?' said the assistant.
'No,' said the man, 'the cucumber was for me
to eat.'
'Can you describe the cucumber?' said the
assistant.
'It was green,' said the man.
'If I said to you,' said the assistant, 'that this
cucumber was found at a ticket barrier, do you

think you could tell me which ticket barrier that might have been? You see we have to make sure that people don't come in here and claim things that don't belong to them. You might come in here and say that you lost a gold watch. I can't hand you a gold watch, just because you say you lost one.'

'I haven't lost a gold watch,' said the man.

'I didn't say that you did,' said the assistant.

'I lost a cucumber,' said the man.

'So you say,' said the assistant.

'Can I ask you if anyone has come in here and handed in a cucumber?' said the man.

'I can tell you that someone has indeed come in here and handed in a cucumber.'

'That'll be mine,' said the man.

'No,' said the assistant, 'what you don't know is whether many people have come in here and handed in cucumbers, in which case we would have the problem of finding out which of the many cucumbers belongs to you.'

'Have many people come in here and handed in cucumbers?' said the man.

'No,' said the assistant.

'Well, that one lone cucumber must be mine,' said the man.

'Not necessarily,' said the assistant, 'someone else could have lost a cucumber and it's their cucumber that was handed in.'

'Oh, yes,' said the man, 'I didn't think of that.'

'Well,' said the assistant, 'if you can't think where you might have left the cucumber, I'm afraid I can't give you the cucumber that we've got here in the lost property office.'

'OK, fair enough,' said the man, 'thanks very much for your help.'

The curtain

There was a kind of curtain or drape. Well,
two actually. I was wearing a jumper and
pushed myself through the gap between
the two curtains. There had been times when
people wanted to keep the two curtains
closed. They had sewn velcro all down the
edges of the curtains. As I pushed through,
I was attacked by the velcro. It grabbed my
jumper, down the sleeves and across my
chest. I lifted my arm and pulled it down again
quickly but the velcro stuck. The curtain
swelled up around me and into my face. I
turned round and the curtain wrapped me up.
The velcro sealed me in. I wrenched my head
back. The curtain folded over my face. I
felt my feet taking off from the floor. I lay
in mid-air and waited for someone to come
and help me. I thought, if I lie very still, I'll
be able to breathe through the curtain that
was lying across my mouth. My arms were
tight next to my sides. The less I move, I
thought, the less I'll need to breathe. I
listened.

Stag

We were on a road between two towns and a sign
came up by the side of the road. It was a picture
of a stag. I've always understood that this means
that as you're driving along a stag could jump out
on to the road. You could hit a stag. Or a stag could
hit you. And maybe the stag would be with other
deer. They could all hit your car. First the stag would
hit it – voom. And then the others – voom voom voom.
We looked into the woods to see if we could see
any. It was raining, so we reckoned that they would
be sheltering under the trees. Or lying under the
bracken. It was autumn, so everything was turning
yellow, brown and dark green. If the stag and deer
were in there, they'd be hard to see. If they came
out and did that voom voom voom thing, you wouldn't
get much warning. In between the woods, there were
open parts, clearings. There was gorse. Again, no
deer. A few cows. A few ponies. Then it was back to
woods: silver birch, oak, beech. As we came round a
corner, I looked again into the woods and saw
something which for a moment looked like a group
or herd of something – a bit grey, a bit brown. Not
deer though. It was jackets. They were hanging from
the trees. Maybe twenty or thirty of them. Damp from
the rain, so they were still. Not that there was any
wind.

Bubbles

When I was a kid, we had a dog that
could wee bubbles. You didn't have to
feed it anything special – not soapy water
or anything like that. What would happen
is that he just got into a certain kind of
mood. You'd see him wandering about
for a bit, he'd walk round in a circle and
then he would stand very still for a moment
and the bubbles would come out. You
could never tell when he would decide
to do it and you couldn't make him do it.
It was just when he felt like it. I told my
friends that he could do it but they didn't
believe me. Then they would come
over and I would say, 'Jack, wee bubbles!'
but he never would. And even if one of them
came over for sleepovers, he wouldn't do it.
So none of them believed me when I said
that he did.

Dog

My friend said, 'Don't buy a dog from a pet shop.'
I said, 'OK.'
He said, 'Good one.'
I said, 'Actually I wasn't thinking of buying a dog.
A few days later I thought I wasn't thinking of buying
a dog but if I was thinking of buying a dog, where
would I go if I was?
My friend had gone to see his relatives in Germany
but I was in the queue at the post office when I
heard a conversation behind me. It was two women.
One of them had a dog.
'I got him at a refuge.'
'Is he clean?'
'Not really.'
I found the address of a dog refuge. It was in the
woods off the motorway. The dogs were in cages.
As I walked past, they came up to the fence and
looked at me. One of them seemed to be laughing
at me. I stopped at another one and looked very
closely at it. Some kind of mongrel. A bit sheepdog.
A bit labrador. It said, 'There's not much point in
getting me. I won't come.'
'Do you get a choice in the matter?' I said.
'Try me,' it said.
'No, no,' I said, 'I'm really not into forcing anyone to
do anything. I'm not even sure I want a dog.'
'Really? It's not our job to help you work out your
hang-ups about dogs, you know,' it said.
'Yes. No. That's right. I wasn't working out anything.'
It went on looking at me very closely.
'Out of interest,' I said, 'why wouldn't you come with
me, if I really wanted you to be my dog?'
'You said it just there,' it said, 'in here I'm part of
something bigger than me. All you can talk about
is "me and my dog", "my dog and me", "what I want,

what I don't want". '

'I could make it bigger than that. When I walk through the park in the morning, there's a meet-up place where dog people all get together with their dogs.'

'Same old crap,' it said, 'we only meet because the people want to meet'.

'Not good?' I said.

'In here, we have a strong sense of being in something together.'

'You are. You're in here together,' I said.

I had a feeling that that wasn't the right thing to say. The dog turned round and walked off to the back of the cage.

Smart chair

I needed a chair. At the shop the man said that there was a new Smart Chair.

He said, 'It anticipates chair use.'

I said, 'So, is it like there's an agreement between me and the chair? I do what it anticipates I'll do.'

He said, 'I think it's more of a prognosis.'

I said, 'I'm afraid I've never known what the difference is between a prognosis and a diagnosis.'

He said, 'I have that problem too.'

I said, 'What about the chair?'

He said, 'I don't think the chair has a problem.'

'That's good,' I said.

He said, 'Would you like to use the chair sir?'

I said, 'I would love to use the chair.'

I sat on it.

'It's very good,' I said.

'How would you describe the sitting experience, sir?'

I said, 'It's... like... sitting. First I sat down and now I'm sitting on.'

He made a note.

He said, 'Would you like a cup of tea or coffee?'

'No thanks,' I said, 'it's a chair I'm after today.'

'I know,' he said.

'And so does the chair, I expect,' I said.

'No, I don't think so,' he said, 'the chair doesn't know that you want to buy a chair.'

Doughnuts

I was having something to eat with a friend of mine.
He took a doughnut out of his bag and started to
eat it. I wanted to know how many people in the world
were biting a doughnut. They would have to be real
doughnuts, not doughnut-like things, like you get in
France and Germany. I thought two and a half
million. My friend said maybe ten million, bearing in
mind it was daytime in the USA. I used to like
doughnuts. I haven't eaten one for twenty years.
My friend ate his doughnut, scrumpled up the paper
bag and asked me if I had a tissue to wipe his mouth.
I said, 'I always have a tissue somewhere on me but I
haven't used a tissue for wiping my mouth after eating
a doughnut for more than twenty years.'
He said, 'Really?'

Eating myself

my auto-immune disease

I was getting weaker. The doctor explained that
I was eating myself. I said I hadn't noticed. When
was I doing this?
'All the time.'
'Am I doing it now?' I said.
He looked at me very closely.
'Yes,' he said.
'I've heard that it's possible to feed a snake with
its own tail. Is it like that?' I said.
'No,' he said, 'you're thinking of "eating" as something
you do with your mouth.'
'Yes,' I said.
'There are other kinds of eating,' he said.
I thought of other holes and apertures in my body
and wondered if anything was going into them. Was
that why I couldn't run anymore? Beating an egg
felt like hard work.
'Your blood swooshes round your body,' he said,
'mostly this is a good thing. In your case, it's not all
good.'
'My blood is eating me?'
'If you didn't have blood, then the bits of you that
are eating you wouldn't get to the bits of you they're
eating.'
'That's accessory to murder,' I said.
'Yes,' he said.
'Can we get at the real culprits?'
'If we get them, the rest of you goes. It would be like
Dresden.'
'Sorry?' I said,
'The bombing killed the civilians not the Nazis.'
'And we're after the Nazis,' I said.
'I'm sorry I mentioned Dresden,' he said, 'it's nothing

like Dresden. Or the Nazis.'

'What about the blood? Are we still talking about the blood?' I said.

'Yes,' he said.

'I think I should be able to beat an egg. I'm 35 years old. A 35 year old should be able to beat an egg. Let's get at these murderers.'

'I'm afraid, it's too late. Very few of them left. They've fed and left. The bit you needed has mostly gone. Think apple core. Chicken bone. Grape pip.'

I thought John Lennon. 'I am the walrus.' I am the grape pip.

'I don't think we need to think in terms of punishment,' he said, 'I sense that you want retribution. It won't help.'

'You bet I want retribution. We're talking killers here. They've crept up on me and eaten me. And they've robbed me.'

'You can't beat an egg. You told me that,' he said.

'So what do you suggest?' I said, 'Something liberal and do-goody? Rehab? Are we going to try the talking cure on my blood?'

'It's simpler than that,' he said, 'do you play football or rugby?'

'Huh!'

'Ah, yes. Do you watch football or rugby?'

I nodded.

'You'll know about subs. We're going to do sub on some players.'

'How do we know that these subs won't eat me?'

'These subs are dead. They can't eat you.'

'They died?'

I felt sorry for the subs. Or sorry for myself.

'Not strictly "dead". Not animate.'

'You're going to send on inanimate subs? And I'll be able to beat an egg?'

'Yes,' he said.

Egg

My brother said that a friend of his said
that he was with some guys who said
that this complete stranger had come
up to them and said that he could boil
an egg using a mobile phone. How did that
work? I said. It seems that this stranger said
that the energy put out by a phone when it's
calling out is not enough to do it, but he
reckoned that he knew a way he could do it
with more than one phone. He said he needed
to borrow phones off four people and
that they should all call each other. But not
any old how. He arranged it so that the four of
them sat round a table. Two of them
sat opposite each other one way, and two of
them sat opposite each other the other way.
As if they were on the ends of a cross.
He then put an egg down in the middle of
the table. Dial up! he said, and one guy
facing one way dialled the guy opposite him
And the guy looking across the table the
other way, dialled the guy opposite him.
Quick, put your phones down close to the
egg, he said. And the four phones made a kind
of box without a lid round the egg. The phones
rang. Let them run, he said. And after about
30 seconds, he said, that should do it. He
lifted up the egg and said, Anyone want to try it?
But before anyone could answer, he said,
I should say that there is a health hazard here.
We've just radiated the egg, and anyone
touching or – god forbid – eating this egg has
increased his chance of getting cancer by
about a million. The guys taking part in the
experiment took a step back. Well, he said,

I'm past caring. Life's not been too good to me, what happens, will happen. You all look in a much better mental state than me. He waited. No one volunteered to try the egg. So he took out a small silver spoon and hit the egg. The rest is history.

Blinking

Two stars were talking to each other.
The bright one said, 'You're blinking.
You keep blinking.'
'I was winking, not blinking,' said the
dull one.
'No, you're blinking. There. And then.
That was a blink. That was definitely
a blink,' said the bright one.
'OK, it was a blink.' said the
dull one, 'OK, OK, OK.'
'No need to get huffy. I'm not
being horrible,' said the
bright one, 'I was just saying.'
'Fine, fine, just leave it,' said
the dull one.
'I am leaving it. I wasn't saying
that there's anything wrong with
blinking. Or winking. If you
want to blink, just blink,' said
the bright one.
'I know, I know, I know,' said
the dull one.
'It's just blinking, it's no big
deal,' said the bright one.
'I know,' said the dull one, 'you're
blinking too.'
'I'm not,' said the bright one.
'What do you mean, you're not?'
said the dull one, 'it's what we do.
We sit up in the sky and we blink.'
'Well maybe you do, but I don't,'
said the bright one.
'It's OK to blink,' said the dull one.
'I know it's OK to blink, I told
you it was OK to blink,' said

the bright one, 'so leave it.'
'I AM leaving it. I wasn't saying
that there's anything wrong with
blinking. Or winking. If you
want to blink, just blink,' said the
dull one.
'I know, I know, I know, I was the
one who was saying that there
wasn't anything wrong with blinking
in the first place,' said the
bright one.
'It's just blinking, it's no big deal,'
said the dull one.
'I know,' said the bright one.

Escalator

I got on a down escalator at a station
and I remember thinking it was
a bit strange that I was the only person
on it. I noticed an ad for kiwi fruit. I
was thinking, that's the first time I've
ever seen an ad for kiwi fruit on the
walls of the escalator and at that
moment I looked ahead to the part
of the escalator where you get off,
where it's like a big metal plate
that you walk on to, off the end of
the escalator.

But it wasn't there. There was no
metal plate. There was just a gap.
A dark space.

I had my bag with me. In it was the
dish I had when I was a baby, the one
with a rim round it. And some papers with
stuff that I had written or was going to
write or had forgotten to write. Looking
ahead at the dark space felt like looking
down a corridor, as if I was at school,
the times I was sent out of class and sat
outside.

Towards the bottom, I remembered there
was the alarm. I thought for a moment
that I might press it. A bell would ring
very loudly and the escalator would
stop. By the time I had thought this, I was
past it.

At the bottom I felt myself going over an edge.
I was in mid-air, floating with the bag.

I heard someone shouting.

Then I landed. I landed on someone.
No, I think it was two people.

Michael Bublé

I was in the loos at one of the big London stations
and I heard someone singing in the next door
cubicle.
I called out, 'Hi! It's Michael Bublé, isn't it?'
'Yep,' he said.
'Can I just say, that you do that really great.'
'Thanks,' he said.
I joined in with him: '...you don't know what
it's like, to love somebody, to love somebody,
the way I love you...'
'I saw you on that Christmas special with Dawn
French,' I said.
'Oh that!'
'Yeah, I know what you mean,' I said, 'a bit, whoaaa!'
'Exactly,' he said.
'Is she like that in real life?' I said.
'Oh yeah, but that's part of the fun, man.'
'Look, I don't want to be rude,' I said, 'but..'
'No you go ahead...'
'But your dancing...'
'I knew you'd bring that up,' he said, 'everyone
does. It's OK, I know what you're going to say...
it looks like I'm just about to fall over. Yeah,
well I am!'
He laughed.
I laughed.
'And would you mind if I said something about
that "You don't know what it's like to love
somebody" track?' I said.
'Go on,' he said.
'I've got Otis Redding's version in my head and...'
'Otis Redding didn't do it. It was the BeeGees,' he
said.
'Are you sure?' I said.
'Oh I'm sure,' he said.

'Well, whoever it was – and it wasn't Otis?'

'It wasn't Otis,' he said.

'Well, the thing is, when you do it, I just keep thinking of – you say, the BeeGees – but whoever it was... and I'm not really listening to you.'

'Hey don't worry about it, man,' he said, 'it's all music.'

'Yes,' I said, 'it's all music. Oh yes and that time you were...'

But I heard the loo flush, the door opened and shut and he was gone.

Expedition

One of the most extraordinary expeditions
of all time occurred in 1854
when a group of explorers left London
on a bright summer's day in July in
search of nothing. The leader of the expedition
was Sir Roland Whisper, a man
who had investigated nothing for longer
than any other person alive. For years
he had pored over maps and charts
with this great task in mind. He gathered
around him a team of fearless adventurers;
London's finest journalists signed up to
Sir Roland's team on the off chance
that they might be the first writers to send
back to London the report that a great
Englishman had discovered nothing.

And so, with their eyes fixed on the
distant horizon, the plucky little expedition
boat sailed out of the Pool of London.
Quayside, wives, friends and well-
wishers bid them godspeed, hoping and
praying that the expedition would be
a success. The sails of the boat
disappeared from view, expectation
was high and though one or two of those
waving goodbye might have been beset
with the occasional doubt, none could
have predicted that not a single member
of the expedition would ever return.

As a result, no one knows whether
Sir Roland's expedition force did or
did not achieve the great prize of
finding nothing.

Indeterminacy

I was thinking about the indeterminacy of being,
and the uncertainty principle. I was wondering
how many times approximation falls short of the
precise point and where or how this intersects
with the universal tendency towards entropy. I
saw people in the street around me burdened
with a sense of inexactitude, people who displace
disappointment onto postponement. Alongside
the road was a light box with the flashing sign
'Delays possible'. I went into a cafe and bought
a falafel wrap, without the chili sauce.

New flats

Some new flats are going up near me. They're overlooking a car park. I don't mean a car park for the flats. It's the big car park for the shopping centre. The idea is that people who live in flats like 'overlooking'. So there are flats overlooking the sea, overlooking rivers, overlooking canals, overlooking railway lines. Now there are flats overlooking car parks. They say that it'll give people something to do: they think that people in the flats will be able to stand on their balconies and watch people parking their cars. Or watch people coming back to the car park, getting into their cars and then driving off. The aim is to build bigger car parks so that more people will park their cars and then they'll build more flats overlooking the car parks and this will build up a sense of being part of something big and interesting – like parking cars. And car parks.

Velcro

The guy next to me on the bus did his jacket up
and said to me, 'When I was a kid, we didn't have
velcro.'
'No,' I said, 'same for me. No velcro.'
'Funny, isn't it?' he said, 'we got along fine with
zips and buttons.'
'Yep,' I said.
'Mind you, not many people know that zips had
to be invented,' he said, 'I mean, if you asked them,
"Were zips invented?", I don't think most people would say
that they were.'
'What about buttons?' I said, 'I like buttons, my mum
had a button box.'
'Do you think most people would know that buttons
were invented?' he said.
'I think so,' I said.
He said, 'I'm not so sure. People take buttons for
granted, these days.'
'The zip on my jacket isn't working,' I said.
He said, 'The thing about velcro is the amount of
time it saves.'
'Really?' I said.
'You bloody bet it does,' he said, 'every time I
velcro up this jacket, I save about three or four
seconds. Imagine what that is across a lifetime.'
'Well, it wouldn't be a lifetime for you, though,' I
said, 'because velcro has come in halfway through
your life, hasn't it?'
'That's right,' he said, 'but think about it from the
kids' point of view. They're saving hours and hours
already. It's why I feel so good about the future,' he
said. 'These kids are going to do so much more
than people of my generation.'
'I think that's what my grandparents thought when
the zip came in,' I said.

'Yes,' he said.

'My grandmother lived for about ten years in America,' I said, 'and she really liked zips.'

'Listen,' he said and pulled the jacket open very quickly, 'every time I do that, I think, it was only a few years ago, you would never have heard that. I can't imagine a world without the sound of velcro.'

'That's not what Paul Simon sang was it?' I said.

'Sang what?' he said.

'No, nothing, "The Sound of Silence", you know.'

'No,' he said. 'There's no velcro in "The Sound of Silence."'

Food cathedrals

One country I was in, the government
had encouraged important people to build what
they called Food Cathedrals. These were giant
shops on the edge of towns and people used
to get in their cars, visit them and wander round
them for hours, thinking of all the food they
would buy if they had the money. Mostly they
didn't but it felt marvelous just being there
walking up and down the aisles, pushing trolleys
and staring at the shelf-fulls of food. Because
people were happy just to do this, without
buying very much, the people running the Food
Cathedrals started getting worried. They weren't
making enough money. So they said they would
set up these things called 'Shops' instead. The
idea here was that instead of all that travelling
and being forced into wandering up and down
aisles to find the food you wanted, these small
'Shops' would be very near to where you lived
and if you couldn't find something, a person
who worked there might tell you where
to find what you wanted. The people running
the Food Cathedrals said that new technology
was able to take all the information about
what the people had bought before, so that they
could tell them what they wanted before they even
knew. This saved them thinking and choosing, they said,
but some people said that they liked the idea of
these 'Shops' where you could get just a little at
a time and it would be like 'fresh' because some of
the Food Cathedral food was on the shelves for
years, people said.

Barbers

I was in the barbers.
When the barber had finished cutting
my hair, he was about to flap my overall
and flick the offcuts on to the floor when
the bloke sitting next to me said,
'Hang on there, can you save that?'
The barber stopped.
'Mm?'
'Yes,' he said, 'just hold it a moment
but can I have that hair?'
We all looked at each other
We looked at my hair sitting on the overall.
The man got up, took off his overall
and went over to his bag. He rummaged
about and took out a box. He
collected up my hair and put it in the box.

I found myself wondering whose hair
it was. Wasn't it mine? Or did it now
belong to the barber? After all, it was
the barber who had cut it off and it
was the barber who was going to
sweep it up and put it in his bin.
I looked at the barber. Though I
remember I looked at the barber in
the mirror, which is not quite the same
as 'looking at the barber'. The barber
said to me, 'Is that OK with you?' I said
to the barber in the mirror, 'Is it OK with you?'
The man went on collecting up my hair.

'What do you want it for?' the barber
asked the man.
'Tea,' he said. 'I make tea with it. This
is very good hair for tea,' he said.

'Most people's hair is no good. This is
very nearly perfect.'

He collected up some more, closed
his box and sat down. I looked at the
barber – face to face this time. We
kind of shrugged with our eyes, didn't
say anything. I paid him, said goodbye
to the man and walked out.

On the way home, I thought, what did
he mean 'very nearly' perfect? Why
wasn't it 'perfect'? I looked at the hair of
of the people on the bus. Is his hair
perfect for making tea? Or hers? Or his?

Footnotes

He noticed that a name appeared several times in footnotes.
The name had, it said, 'provided some information'. In another
place, the name had, it said, 'been present'. In yet another, the
name had, it said, 'offered an amusing opinion'. The name was
never in full, always with initials; the surname spelled slightly
differently – sometimes with an 'l' sometimes not. I tried to
find out more: I googled, I sent emails to people who
would have been or could have been mutual acquaintances;
I wrote to places where the name might have been educated. It
was always nothing. Polite apologies but no information available.
I began to doubt if the person existed. What if the name had at
first been invented as a witness in order to bulk up a tenuous
proposition, or serve as evidence to a story that wasn't entirely
true? What if there had followed, since then, a process of
quotation of quotation but authors had failed to mention the
middleman? Or was there a knowing joke passing between people
whereby the name could serve as an available backup of the
truth of any old event or conversation: the name 'was there', the
name 'had seen' it, the name 'could vouch' for it? I made contact
with authors who had cited the name and received evasive replies:
papers were now 'in archive' and the author 'didn't have time' now
'to pull them out'; or, 'yes, there had been an intermediary' but it
seemed at the time 'pedantic to mention it'; the 'exact citation' had
been taken from a radio programme which 'hadn't been
preserved', and so on and so on. One person said that she had met
the name as 'part of her original research'. I arranged a meeting
in a cafe in Paddington. She didn't turn up. I tried again. She
was 'in the midst of moving'. I tried again. Her mother 'was dying'.
I tried again. She had re-married and her husband 'preferred
her not to have contact with previous liaisons'. Around this time,
I noticed in one book that a quote I had seen attributed to the
name was attributed to someone else. I wrote to that person. That
person said that it was indeed something he said and he had 'never
heard of' the name. In fact, it was something this person was quite
proud of having said and suspected that the name was someone

who had 'wished he had said it himself'. Now the name seemed to be taking on a motive: envy; he was bitter. Yes, that was it, he must have felt excluded... and had found a way in by adopting the clever sayings of others. No! Surely he was the opposite: he acknowledged that deep down he was the little guy but to be a footnote was in some ways a big thing. Two footnotes was bigger. Three footnotes – massive. Somewhere in a one room flat, the name was sitting surrounded with books and articles in which he was a footnote.

The frown

I was waiting for the dentist and the receptionist said,
Why the frown? I said I didn't really know and it was
something I started doing when I was about ten. People
noticed it even then. Maybe I thought it looked serious
and I wanted to be as serious as my brother or my father.
Don't we often want to be more than we are? I said, the
plus side being that it helps us carry on, but the down side
being that we are always unsatisfied, but then, that doesn't
spring up as if by magic from inside, our desire is manufactured,
teams of people sit in towers of steel and glass figuring out
how they can get us to want stuff and even if we can't afford it,
we still yearn for it, and isn't it this the reason why we stick
with the system, eh, we'd rather have what we can't have, than
change the fact that we can't have it? She said she was
just wondering if I was bothered about the time of the next
appointment.

The garden

I was in this garden centre and an announcement
came over the tannoy that we weren't allowed to
pick any of the fruit off the fruit trees. There was a
woman there who was standing next to a tree and
one of the guys who served in the garden centre
asked her if she wanted an apple off the tree he was
looking after. She said no. She asked me if I wanted
one. I said no. Then the voice came over the tannoy
and said, 'Oi, you two, you've ruined everything.
You, the woman, you're supposed to have taken an
apple off the man there. And then you were supposed
to have offered it to the man there.' The woman
shrugged and walked off. I picked up a pot of
lavender and went to pay for it.

Pelicans

My Mum told me that
when I was two
she took me to St James's Park
to see the pelicans.

I looked in books at pelicans.
Great big pelicans
with beaks like shopping bags.

She said:
one day we'll go back to
St James's Park to see the pelicans.

I said:
Yes, let's.

But we never did.
We never went to St James's Park
to see the pelicans.

Sixty years after the time
my mum took me to St James's Park
to see the pelicans
I went.
On my own.

I walked over to the water.
I so wanted to see the pelicans.
I looked
But there were none.
No pelicans.

So I walked along by the side of the water
And I thought of me being two years old
And my mother being thirty years old.

And I walked over a little bridge
And I looked out across the water
And there was a pelican.
And another
And another
And so they were there:
the pelicans
standing with their beaks
like shopping bags
waiting for me
to come back and see them
with my mother.

The dryer

It was late and before going home I thought
I'd nip into a cafe for a cup of tea and a
sandwich. I found one down an alley near
the station. They had run out of pretty nearly
everything but I got a tomato sandwich and
before I ate it, I went to the toilet.
I washed my hands and turned on the
hand dryer. What came out was a pretty
poor flow of air. Coming out in short bursts.
And it wasn't very warm. And actually, it was
a bit damp. I was just about to leave the toilet
when I heard a cough. It seemed very near.
Like from behind the wall. Or in the wall. As
the cough came out, a bit more of the dryer
blew air. Then stopped. I thought that was
odd and I looked more closely at the dryer.
I touched it and it wobbled. So I got hold of it,
and shook it. I don't think I pulled it but it came
away in my hands. I had the whole dryer in
my hands. On the other side of the dryer, in
the hole left in the wall, was a man. His face,
that is. The man's face. He was standing
behind the wall, or in the wall, with his face
behind the dryer. All I could see of him was
his face. I said, 'Did you just...' And before
I could finish, he said, 'Yep, that was me.'

O'Neill's

I went into O'Neill's on the Euston Road and said,
'Did anyone hand in a hat thing?'
The guy said, 'May have done, I'll look.'
He looked under the counter and pulled out a box.
It was full of hats and scarves. I fished around in them.
'No, none of those,' I said.
'What colour was it?' he said.
'Blue, light blue.'
'What – a woollen one, was it?'
'Yes,' I said.
'You said it was a "hat thing", do you mean it wasn't
really a hat?'
I nodded.
'What? More like a balaclava?'
'Yes, exactly. That's right. A balaclava.'
'Nope. I haven't seen it. Maybe Danuta has. She was
on last night. When were you in?'
'About fifty years ago.'
'Mm?'
'I'm just working it out... I must have been around
18 or 19, I was a student. Mostly, my parents left
me to get on with it but...'
'You've come in here to get a hat... that...'
'...every now and then my mother would look at me
and say, "You need a belt", and she'd get me a belt.
And then one time she said, "You need a hat", and
she got me this blue hat.'
'I haven't seen my mother in years,' he said.
'The thing is,' I said, 'I was upstairs. It was a meeting.
Some kind of meeting.'
'I should call her,' he said, 'but hey – I don't.'
'We were going to solve everything. Change the
world.'
'And you left your hat.'
'Yep.'
We looked in the box. I fished around again.
'It's not here,' I said.

Walking

When I was in hospital, once I started to get
better they would let me get up and walk
about. I used to walk out of my ward, and
down the corridors. Bit by bit I was getting
stronger. One time I got to the end of one
corridor that I hadn't walked down before and
there was a ward in front of me. I was
feeling a bit bored so I thought I would
just pop in and have a look. I noticed
that it was very quiet. For a moment I
wondered if everyone in the ward had
died. It was all so still. Instead of walking
out – which is what I should have done –
I went further into the ward. The beds
were all where they normally are, all
along the walls, some with drips or
machines of some kind. None of the
beds were empty but instead of people
in them, there were chess pieces. Not
ordinary chess pieces. Human-size ones.
They just lay in the beds. Not moving.
Or making any sound. Pawns, knights,
kings, queens and the rest. I thought
that I would be able to figure out some
kind of order to it: kings and queens in
some kind of special beds, or maybe the
pawns would be the nurses or the cleaners
but no, it was nothing like that. It was
just that there were all the different chess
pieces in the beds. Though now I think
about it, I don't remember seeing a
bishop. There should have been four.
But I don't remember there being even
one of them.

Lions

All is not what it seems
Sometimes what's real
is less real than our dreams.

We are four lions
Are we asleep?
Or not moving
with our eyes shut?

Are we fixed and stuck
as still as stone
Or do we blink?
Do we speak?
Do we think?

We have heard you talk of a far-off land
where creatures like us run and hunt
We have heard you talk of a pride of lions
where creatures like us sleep in the sun.

We hear your feet on the steps of the Fitz
trip-trap, amble, clamber or run
We hear you complain of wind and rain
We hear you laugh when you see the sun.

We hear you talk of war and peace
voices that come, voices that go
we hear of pockets full or empty,
what you say is what we know

We hear lovers' whispers as you walk by
and sighs of sadness from deep inside
We hear sounds of fear in how you breathe
the hug of hope and the smile of pride.

We hear you wonder about our eyes
We hear you study our hard stone faces.
We hear you wonder if we slumber
like lions after hunting in far-off places

We hear our dreams of other times
not then, or now, or here, or there
We hear a dream of how we rise
and breathe in the living air.

And we all four together as lions
walk the street, none last or first
to find the water that is ours
to help us quench this terrible thirst.

The map

Sometimes, when it's cold or things haven't been going well, I go to a nearby station and stand in front of the map. Not the one for the rail routes. The map that shows the station amongst the local streets. On the map there's an arrow and it says, 'You are here'. I stand and look at the arrow and read, 'You are here'. Then I go home.

Memory stick

I bought a memory stick and put some files on it.
When I opened it up, I saw that it had hundreds of thousands
of files on it.
I opened a file called 'Melon' and it said that I had eaten a melon
near the Colosseum in Rome and that I swallowed the pips. I
don't think that can be right. I don't think I would have swallowed
the pips. I know why I wouldn't have swallowed the pips: it's
because my mother always said that she got appendicitis as a
result of swallowing melon pips. I looked that up on the memory
stick to see if it had that bit of memory. It was there. It said,
'Mother talking about getting appendicitis from eating melon pips'.
I'm not sure where this leaves me. Should I go with the memory
I have of not eating melon pips? Or should I trust that the memory
stick has got it right? I mean, I can remember the melon
outside the Colosseum in Rome. It was summer and too hot
for me. There was a guy selling melons. I remember eating the
melon. I don't remember how I got into the melon. Did he open
it up and whip the pips out? Or did he just hand it to me and
I opened it up with that knife I always took around with me?
And I know how to do that thing where you whip the seeds out,
cut the melon into crescents, run the knife between the skin and
the flesh, cut the crescents of melon into sections, then
stick the point of the knife into one section at a time, so that
you can eat the melon, chunk by chunk. But no seeds. That's
the point. No one wants to eat the seeds. My mother used to
collect them, wash them and make necklaces out of them.
That one's on the memory stick. I guess it got muddled between
the necklace and some baloney about me eating the seeds.

Paper plane

for Simon Armitage

When I was a kid
I once made a paper plane
that was so big
I went for a ride on it.

What happened was that
I was at the park
and I threw it
and as I let go
I jumped on it.

I flew over the bit
where we played football
and then over the pond
with the island in the middle.
What was great was the way
people looked up at me
and waved.

I loved the way they waved.
It made me feel good
the way they waved.
The day hadn't been good
up till then.
I had had an arithmetic test.
It didn't go very well.

The landing wasn't too good though.
The plane came down hard
and crumpled.
You know how paper crumples up.
That's what happened.

I wasn't what you might say was 'hurt'.
Just a bit shaken up.

Some people came over and
asked me if I was alright.
I said, 'Yeah, I'm fine.'
Someone said, 'You're not going
to leave all that paper there, are you,
sonny?'
I shrugged.
A woman helped me crumple it up
really small
and we put it in
a bin.

Then I went home.

My dad said,
'How did the arithmetic test go?'
'Not too good,' I said.

Messengers

The king's idea was that there should be a messenger
service all over his kingdom. Whoever wanted to send
a message would hire one of the king's messengers.
There would be a fee for this of 100 crowns a year which
would be paid straight to the king, into his coffers to pay
for wars. For a hundred crowns you could hire a
messenger any time you liked. The king announced that
the messenger service had begun. Twenty messengers
waited in the yard outside the king's palace. Nothing
happened. Nothing happened for several days. The
leading messenger went to see the king.
'I don't think this messenger thing is going to work,' he
said. 'Anyone wanting to send a message – apart from you,
sir – is going to have to come here first.'
'Yes,' said the king, 'that's why it's a good idea.'
'No, sir,' said the chief messenger, 'you see by the time the
person wanting to send a message has come here, they
might just as well have sent someone from where they
are.'
'That's a good point,' said the king.
'Might I suggest that the messengers do routes?' said the
chief messenger.
'Go on,' said the king.
'One of us does route A to B. One of us does route C to D.
Another does route E to F and so on. People who want
messages sent come to the messenger point, A or C or E
and so on.'
And that's what happened. The people who wanted to send
messages came to the messenger points and the messengers
ran the routes. It became very popular. The money rolled in.
The king waged wars. Everyone was happy. The messenger
system got more popular. The messengers worked very hard
running between the messenger points. Some days, they didn't
have time to eat. They said that the king had to take on more
messengers. He said he couldn't do that as he needed more

soldiers. The messenger service stopped being so good. One day it was because some message-senders gave their messages to the messenger but the messenger never got to the person the message was being sent to. No one knew what happened to him. He just disappeared. Some said that he dropped dead because he hadn't eaten for a month. Some said that he met someone on the way and decided to stay with her for the rest of his life. Someone said that he stopped off at a theatre, stole a wig, a false beard and a magician's cloak and was now touring the country doing conjuring tricks. Another day it was because the messenger had so many messages to remember that he muddled them up: someone who was supposed to have got a message saying that he loved her more than the night-sky loves the stars, ended up getting threatened with having her legs broken for not paying her rent. A birthday greeting went to someone who was dead. One day, one of the message points was full of people wanting to send messages but there was no messenger to take them. The people ended up telling their messages to each other. At least four people ended up getting married as a result but for the rest it was a disaster. In the end the chief messenger went to see the king.

'The message system is not working,' he said. 'You haven't got enough messengers.'

'That's where you're wrong,' said the king. 'It's not "not enough messengers", it's "too many messages". Yack, yack, yack,' said the king, 'that's all you do. What's the weather like where you are? How's Auntie? How's the little one? Did you see so-and-so last night? What are you wearing? Where are you? I'm on the chariot on the way to the sea, where are you? On and on and on and on.'

'But you're still collecting the hundred crowns off people,' said the chief messenger.

'Of course, I am,' said the king, 'I've got wars to do.'

Station

I was on a station and I needed to get somewhere
quickly. I went up to the guy in uniform, showed him
the name of the place on a bit of paper. He looked
up at the notice board and said,
'You won't be able to get there now.'
I said, 'I'm stuck then.'
'You haven't got any bags, have you?' he said.
'No.'
'I'll tell you what I can do for you,' he said, 'I have got a
platform over here,' and he flicked his head to the right.
'Really?'
'This is just between me and you, OK?'
'Sure,' I said.
'Just follow me.'
He took me along to the end of platform 12 and then
ducked down behind a shed. He pulled me down with
him. He nodded towards the next platform and put his
finger up to his lips. I kept quiet. He looked at his watch.
'OK,' he whispered, and then beckoned me to follow
him again. We climbed down off the platform and
walked across several sets of railway lines. Trains were
passing. I wanted to tell him that I was only going to
visit my brother and it could wait. I kept close behind
him. I like railway lines shining when the light is fading.
I wondered how many lines there were. Not just railway
lines but lines above, cutting through the sky. We were
some way off from the station by now. We were walking
by the side of a hoarding. I was next to a woman's legs.
A giant woman. With giant legs. He took me round behind
the hoarding. There was a single track.
'Wait there,' he said, 'and you'll be alright. Remember,'
he said, 'nothing about this to anyone, OK?'
'Sure,' I said, 'when will the train go?' I said.
He looked at his watch.
'Later,' he said, 'yep, later.'

The world's best museum

We were on holiday in the country and just
outside a village that we were going through we
saw a sign that said, 'The World's Best
Museum'. I said that I thought it strange that
if it was the 'world's best museum' we hadn't
heard of it. And anyway, why would it be
here? That made everyone angry, and they
said that there must be something wrong with
me to put such a downer on everything.
So I said, fair enough, let's go. We went down
several country lanes and over one of those
level crossings that everyone worries about
and got to a house that stood on its own
next to some woods. The sign outside just
said, 'Museum'. It didn't say what it was a
museum of. There were no lights on and it
was just beginning to get dark, so I said that
I didn't think anyone was in but the others
said there may be and that was me putting
a downer on things again. So we knocked on
the door and quite quickly a woman came out
and asked us if we had come for the wood. We
said that we hadn't. We had come for the
museum. She looked a bit puzzled for a moment
so I said, 'The sign. The Museum.'
'Ah yes, the Museum,' she said, 'the Museum.'
She said to follow her through the house and
out the back. In the garden there were some
sheds and she said, 'There you go.'
We moved forward, a bit hesitantly, and went
up to the first shed. I pulled at the door and it
came open after a strong tug. Inside it was
dark, so we gathered around the doorway and
looked in. I could make out a sign on a shelf at
the back of the hut. It said, 'What do you reckon?'

The little one said, 'What does it say?'
I said, "What do you reckon?"
She said, 'I don't know.'
I said, 'I don't know either.'
Then the woman from the Museum said,
'What do you reckon?'
And I said, 'Do you mean, what do I reckon
with "What do you reckon?" or do you
just mean, "What do you reckon?"'
She looked at me and said, "What do
you reckon?"'
The little one said that she didn't like
it. I said that it looked like there were
more sheds we could go in but the others
said that there wasn't much point.
I said that this time it wasn't me putting
a downer on things.
They said, 'Never mind that.'
The little one said, 'We don't have to
go through the level crossing on the way
back, do we?'

Connie Rosen

My mother loved museums.
She said that the Bethnal Green Museum saved her.
I wondered what it saved her from.
When my father swore in Yiddish
she said, 'Don't say that!'
I said, 'What did he say?'
She said, 'Don't tell him.
It sounds like my uncles in the back room,
playing gin rummy.'
I said, 'What's gin rummy?'

In one museum she went to,
she saw a sampler.
A nine year old girl had embroidered it
hundreds of years ago.
After that, we would be having tea
and my mother would look up and say,
'Let self-sacrifice be its own reward.'
I said, 'What's self-sacrifice?'

My father went out the room.
We heard him upstairs.
My mother said, 'Ask your father
what he's doing, and tell him
to stop it.'

She walked into my bedroom.
She said, 'This place is a mishadamonk,'
I said, 'What's a mishadamonk?'
'Your bedroom,' she said.

She loved poems or bits of poems.
The rest of us would be talking and
she'd suddenly say in a tragic voice:
'Tread softly because you tread on my dreams.'
Or she would look out of the window and shout,
'I'm a cat who likes to gallop about doing good.'

On the news they said,
'Don't eat the corned beef.
The corned beef comes from South America.
There's a typhoid outbreak in South America.
Don't eat the corned beef.'
My mother went to the cupboard.
It was stacked up with corned beef tins.
She took one out.
'Better not open that
till the typhoid outbreak's
over,' she said.

Hands

Here is my right hand
Here is my left hand
Let's say my mother is my right hand
my father is my left.

And this is me.

My mother is born in the
East End Mothers' Lying-in Home
on the Commercial Road, in London.

My father is born in Brockton, Massachusetts
in the USA.

I was born in Harrow in London.

My mother told a story
of how at school they asked the children
to bring in flowers but she lived in a flat
over a shop and they didn't have flowers.

My father told a story
of how his mother went to a charity
to ask for shoes for him
but they said no because she was married.
True, but married to a man she'd left behind
in Brockton – or he left her
and never saw him again.
No matter. No shoes.

And here's me:
my mother and father helped me learn
my mother and father helped me learn how to learn
and I've done OK – better than OK
I don't have to beg for shoes
I have all the flowers I want and more.

So shall I say
I don't need my right hand
I don't need my left hand?
Shall I turn my back on my hands?

There –
I've done it.

But they're still there.
I hear them telling another story.
Told to them in the language of their grandparents

How strong is one matchstick?
They can break one matchstick.
How strong is two matchsticks?
They can break two matchsticks.
How strong is a whole box of matchsticks?
They can't break a whole box of matchsticks.

That's how we must be.
We have to be:
all the matchsticks.

Here is my right hand
Here is my left hand

This is me.

Plastic pot

Sometime after my father died, my step-mother came
over with a small plastic pot. One of the things in it was
a brass brooch of a miner's lamp. I had never seen it
before. I went online to see what it was. I found out
that they were sold by the miners' union during and
after the General Strike of 1926. It was to help the
miners' families who were starving. I remembered
my father saying that he could remember the General
Strike from when he was 7. Something about a type-writer
being thrown over a wall. He hadn't ever mentioned the
brooch. It must have been his mother's. He didn't know
his father. His father was in the US. My father, my father's
sister and my father's mother didn't live near any pits and
coalfields. They lived in Whitechapel, in east London. In
a house with 6 or 7 others. I don't think anyone in
the house knew any miners. My father said that sometimes
sailors used to come to the house. He remembered a sailor
who came from Jamaica.

Coffee tables

My father made coffee tables. He went to school furniture
dumps and brought home chemistry laboratory benches.
He turned them into coffee tables by sawing the legs down
so that the bench top was just a few inches off the floor.
He went to junk shops and discovered the marble tops
of old tables that were used in bedrooms as poor people's
bathrooms. He brought them home, threw away the
wooden base and fixed black square metal legs to the
marble tops. He brought back a staffroom table. He
sawed the legs down and hired a floor sander to
sand down the top. He walked up and down the
table top till all the scratches had gone. My mother
said that he made coffee tables so that he could have
somewhere to put his droppings. 'He never picks anything
up. He only ever puts things down.'

Some days there were so many coffee tables in the place,
it was difficult to get round the room. When we left home,
he gave my brother and me some of the coffee tables.
One time he came over with a coffee table that he had
bought for me. It looked like an old coffee table but it had
only just been made. One of my children stuck a red sign
saying 'DANGER' on it.

The ceiling

After my mother died, my father lay in bed looking
up at the ceiling. He heard a shuffling sound, the
movement of paper over paper, books falling.
A continuous sound. Relentless. The ceiling
trembled and bulged. At the sides, where it
met the walls, the ceiling inched downwards.
It juddered. He lay in the bed watching it getting
nearer. He knew it was the weight of the papers
and books that was forcing the ceiling down.
Nothing could stop it. He could have got out.
He could have escaped. He didn't. He waited.
He knew the ceiling wouldn't stop. He knew
he couldn't stop it.

Shoe horn

My grandmother left America on a boat for Liverpool
with 3 children she had had in Brockton, Massachusetts.
She left behind in Brockton the 2 children she'd had in
Whitechapel in London. People said she didn't say
goodbye to the children she left in America.
They were hoeing in a field, so she waved. One of them
she never saw again. No one knows how she said goodbye
to her husband, their father. People said that he told her
he'd join her soon. He never did. When she got back,
one of the children she brought with her, died. I remember
her coming to see us. My father called her 'Ma'. No one
round our way called their mother, 'Ma'.
'I've got something for you,' she said.
She put her hand in her bag. It was a shoe horn, made
of metal, painted red. In winter the red shoe horn
was cold.

The Battle of Stalingrad, 1950s

My mother, Connie Rosen, née Isakofsky
fought at the Battle of Stalingrad
on our kitchen table.
Her hands moved to and fro
round the plates, in and out of the salt and pepper.

She told it so that it was thanks to Stalingrad
the whole world had survived;
her dreams that the world could be better
had survived;
she had survived.

My aunt

My aunt didn't have pets but she looked after two gloves. Indoors, it was no big deal, we hardly noticed that she sat with the gloves beside her on the sofa. You'd sometimes see her patting them or stroking them. They had their own chair at the table. When she came to the door to say goodbye she nearly always had them sitting folded over her arm. It really was no big deal. The only time it was more of a thing was when she came over to our place. She brought the gloves with her in a cat basket. When she arrived, she put the basket down on the floor and slid the gloves out of the cat basket. They were with her all the time she was at our house, then when she went home she eased the gloves back into the cat basket. The basket was always on the seat beside her in the car. As she drove off, we waved to her. I think there was once or twice I waved to the gloves.

Burnt down

My mother said that the night I was born, the
church burnt down. I told people: 'The night
I was born the church burnt down.' I heard
people say it, 'The night he was born, the
church burnt down.'
I thought that I did it. I burnt the church down.
All through my childhood, the remains of
the church stood next to the back yard
and alley out the back of the shops
where we lived. We used to climb in to
the burnt out church and look for treasures:
melted coloured glass. It felt good to
know that something good came out of
what I had done.

They shall not pass

*first read at an attempted march through Whitechapel
by the EDL in 2011*

You Connie Ruby Isakofsky
from Globe Road in Bethnal Green
You Harold Rosen
from Nelson street, Whitechapel
You Connie with your mother and father
from Romania and Poland
You Harold with your family from Poland.

You Connie
You Harold
your families working in the *shmatte* trade
Hats, caps, jackets and gowns
Hats, caps, jackets and gowns.

You both saw Hitler on the Pathe News
You both saw Hitler blaming the Jews
You both collected for Spain,
collecting for Spain
when Franco came.

When round the tenements,
the whisper came
Mosley wants to march
here, through the East End.

So what should it be?
To Trafalgar Square to support Spain:
No pasaran?

Or to Gardiner's Corner to support Whitechapel
They shall not pass.

Round the tenements
the whisper came
Fight here in Whitechapel
the whisper came:
Winning here
we support
Spain there.

These are the streets where we live
These are the streets where we go to school
These are the streets where we work.

They shall not pass.

You Connie
You Harold
went to Gardiner's Corner
You went to Cable Street
You piled chairs on the barricades
The mounted police charged you
A stranger took you indoors
so you could escape a beating
And thousands
hundreds of thousands came here
fighting Mosley
supporting Spain
thinking of Nazi Germany.

And
Mosley did not pass.

You Connie
You Harold
said, today the bombs on Guernica in Spain
tomorrow the bombs on London here.
And you were bombed
the same planes, the same bombs
landing in the same streets
where you had said
'they shall not pass'.

And the bodies
piled up across the world
Million after million after million after million
You Connie, your cousins in Poland
taken to camps
wiped out
You Harold, your uncles and aunts in France and Poland
taken to camps
wiped out.

But you Connie, my mother
you Harold, my father
you survived
you lived
we were born
we grew.

You mother
You father
told us these things
I write these things
And today,
I tell you these things
We remember here together
Thanks to you
And we say:
'They shall not pass'.

Not just for them

a story for Holocaust Memorial Day

This is about France
This is about Germany
This is about Jews.
This is not about France
This is not about Germany
This is not about Jews.

In the family they were always the French uncles,
the ones who where there before the war,
the ones who weren't there after the war.
The family said that one of them was a dentist
and the other one mended clocks and that's it.
Not quite it. There was a street that the relatives
here and in America kept saying, which was:
rue de Thionville, rue de Thionville.
And places in France: Nancy, Metz, Strasbourg
and one of the brothers was Oscar and the other was Martin.
And that was it. Though Olga, in America
nearly as small as a walnut, said that she used
to write letters to them to learn how to write French.
And Michael here in England said that he used to
write letters to them to learn how to write French.
And that was it. That's how it was, they said.
Michael knew how it was. His mother was the sister
of the French uncles and she waved Michael goodbye
when he was 17 and that was the last he saw of her.
And that was it. But I wouldn't let it go and I
started looking for the rue de Thionville and at an
airport I met a guy who came from Metz and he said
he would go to the Mairie, the town hall, and look
up Oscar and Martin, rue de Thionville and he did
or says he did and he wrote back to say he didn't find
anything. And that was that. But then Teddy in America

wrote to say that some letters have turned up, a son
of a brother of a mother or something has got letters
from 1941. And they're from Oscar, and they're from Michael's father
And oh my god they're asking for help, they're letters
to their brother Max. (Look, I know the names won't mean much to you,
I've been living with this stuff and I don't even know why
I've tried so hard to find out about it, but there were these
brothers and sisters, all born in Poland, one of them is
Michael's mother. That's Stella, she stayed there,
married Bernard, there are the ones who went to France
that's Oscar and Martin; there's Max who went to America
along with Morris that's my father's father. I know the names.)
So when I see the letters I know who they are, Oscar asking Max
for help, Bernard asking that money should be sent to Michael
who was now in Siberia, Bernard doesn't know that he'll never see
his son Michael again, and I'm looking at the letters, and there's
an address in France, not rue de Thionville, in Metz
or Nancy or Strasbourg. It's 11 Rue Mellaise, (remember that)
in Niort in Deux-Sèvres. The other side of France.
And I start to read about how they all fled, everyone fled
'L'exode' they called it, the Exodus, everyone fled from the east
to the west, and here's Oscar in the west in Niort
Deux-Sèvres...11 Rue Mellaise, (remember the address).
I find the house on Google, there it is, a shop downstairs
a flat above, the French street, the shutters, the grey
render of the walls, the kind of place I've walked down
a thousand times on trips to the country I love to be in,
the place I discovered things I couldn't buy or have
in England in the 1960s: 'jus de pomme' in big brown bottles,
fresh melons, blue vests, 'espadrilles', I didn't even
know why it mattered and here was 11 Rue Mellaise,
the kind of place I would have liked to have stayed in
but this was the address for the last letter any of us have
from Oscar. And that was that. But I wouldn't let go
of it, and I started looking for what happened to Jews
in Niort, in Deux-Sèvres and I found books which spoke of
'rafles', round-ups and a young rabbi who did all he could.
But it wasn't enough and every time I found a book
I went to the index to look for the name, Rosen. It's

something I've done, looking for my own name, or
the name of my brother or father or mother but now
I was looking for Oscar or Martin, and then, somewhere
I found something that I should have known about but
didn't. '*Le fichier juif*', the Jewish file, the document or dossier of
Jews. In France, there's a job called 'Prefect' and 'Sub-prefect',
local officials and these prefects and sub-prefects
carefully wrote out the names of every Jew, date of birth,
place of birth, job, married to... names of children. And there
in one of the books was page 1 of the *fichier juif* for
Deux-Sevres. But where was this *fichier juif*? I wanted to
know, I don't know why, and it seems as if most of the
fichiers juifs just disappeared after the war, they just
slipped away and would have been lost, vanished.
But for some reason a pile of them turned up in a
basement of a building and carefully and slowly
they had been put together and copied but all I
could see was page one. A facsimile of page one.
And that was that. But then at the back of a book
I found the name of another book: '*Les chemins
de la honte, itinéraire d'une persecution, Deux-Sèvres
1940-1944*', by Jean-Marie Pouplain... *The Path of Shame
the Account of a Persecution, Deux-Sèvres 1940-1944*
and I ordered it. It arrived into a house we were
on the verge of moving out of, so there was
something temporary and on the move about
us at that point, but the book arrived and I pulled
off the cardboard packaging and I did what I've done before.
I looked in the index for Rosen and it said, 34, 65,
96, 108, 197, 202, 203, 205, 210, 212, 213, 236, 240, 244.
And I turned to page 34 and there was the *fichier juif*
and number 40, it said, '*Rosen, Jeschie, né le 23 juin,
1895, polonaise, bonneterie, marié à Kesler, Rachel,
née en 1910, 11 Rue Mellaise.*'
Some things very right, some things not so right.
The name Jeschie, Oh I figured it was a nickname.
Jews have Hebrew names and sometimes their Christian
names are echoes of the Hebrew names, perhaps he was
Oscar because it rhymed with Yehoshua and the Yiddish

nickname of Yehoshua was perhaps Jeschie...?
But the job, 'bonneterie' it means the person who sells clothes
in the market. Not a dentist or a clockmaker. And I slowly
looked up each number and each page number told what
the prefect and the sub-prefect carefully wrote down, how
Jeschie and Rachel were given their yellow stars, how they
had to pin a sign saying '*Entreprise Juive*', '*Jüdisches Geschäft*',
Jewish Business to their market stall, how everything they owned
was taken away from them in a process called 'aryanisation'.
The business was Aryanised...whatever that meant, and there
on one of the entries it said that Jeschie was an '*horloger de
carillon*' – a mender of chiming clocks. But what about the
last pages? and I turned to the last page numbers –
pages 234 and 236, 240 and 245 and Jeschie Rosen
was arrested outside of Deux-Sèvres, he seems to have tried
to get away, '*clandestinement*' – secretly, but was picked up
somewhere else and then he and Rachel appear on another
document, the lists that the Nazis made in Paris of every Jew
they put on what the French called '*convois*' – 'convoys'
and there they are on convoy 62, leaving Paris on November
20 1943 going to Auschwitz.

And when I had read all that, as I stood there with the book
in my hand I knew that I was the first person in the family to know
all this and it felt like I had to tell everyone and I sat down
and started to write a letter to all the relatives which I
didn't finish because I had to go and find out – and I knew
where to look – how many people were on that convoy, how long
did it take to get to Auschwitz, what happened the moment
the train arrived, how many never came back, how many
survived.

I read: '1200 Jews left Paris/Bobigny at 11.50 am on
November 20 1943. Arrived Auschwitz November 25, as cabled
by SS Colonel Liebenhenschel 1181 arrived.
There had been 19 escapees, they were young people
who escaped at 8.30pm Nov 20 near Lerouville.
In the convoy there were 83 children who were less than 12 years old.
Out of the convoy 241 men were selected for work and given numbers
164427-164667.
Women numbered 69036-69080 were selected too.
914 were gassed straightaway.
In 1945, there were 29 survivors – 27 men 2 women.'

I looked over what I wrote before I sent it off to my brother,
and to my cousins who would pass it on to Michael and to Max's
son in America – who I haven't told you is 103 years as I write this.
I thought about what kind of war was it, what kind of people
was it, who looked at a mender of clocks and his wife and put
them in a document, made them wear a yellow star, made them
put a sign up on their market stall, took their money away
from them, arrested them, put them in a transit camp,
put them on a train and sent them to a camp in Poland
where they were killed?

This is a story about France,
a story about Germany, a story about Jews.
This is a story
that's not about France, not about Germany,
not about Jews.
I found these things out in order to know. I found these
things out, I know now, in order to tell other people.
I found these things out so that Jeschie and Rachel will be known.
But in the end I know that the point of them being known is
that this is a story not just for them and about them.

Mme Le Pen

the reason why
they gave a yellow star
to my father's uncle and aunt

the reason why
they told them they had to fix a sign
saying 'Jewish Business' on their market stall

the reason why
they fled from their refuge in the rue Mellaise
in Niort

the reason why
they took refuge in Nice

the reason why
they were arrested and transported
to Paris, to Drancy, to Auschwitz and to their death

is because the officials of Vichy
made a 'Jewish File' of foreign Jews
and gave it to the Nazis
at the exact moment
that the Resistance was welcoming
Jews and was welcoming foreigners

and that's the reason why
I am telling you these things
Mme Le Pen.

Mme Le Pen

la raison pourquoi
on a donné une étoile jaune
à l'oncle et à la tante de mon père

la raison pourquoi
on a demandé qu'ils devaient attacher
une affiche disante 'Entreprise juive'
à leur étal de marché

la raison pourquoi
ils ont fui leur asile
dans la rue Mellaise à Niort

la raison pourquoi
ils se sont réfugiés à Nice

la raison pourquoi
on les a arrêtés et on les a transportés
à Paris, à Drancy, à Auschwitz et à leurs morts

est parce que
les officiers de Vichy
ont fait un 'Fichier juif' des juifs étrangers
et l'a donné aux Nazis au moment exacte
que la Résistance a dit bienvenu aux juifs
bienvenu aux étrangers

et c'est ça, la raison pourquoi
je vous dis ces choses
Mme Le Pen.

Morning after the killings in Paris

Monday morning in Bletchley-like Intelligence bunker. Around a large table, sits a group of Oxford educated men in their forties and fifties. A senior-looking figure speaks:

'Morning chaps, first off, I think yesterday's press conference was a great success. There were some excellent photo ops and we were looking good. But must move on. Let's do some blue sky envelope pushing and ask the biggie: Why do these men take up arms and shoot people? Straight off, can we rule out stuff that we can't do anything about – so if you come back at me and say some rot about "wars" – I'll say to you, "not our department". If you say, "oh these young men have very little chance to do anything worthwhile or make their lives feel better unless they can win the lottery, sell drugs, take drugs or rob a bank", I'll say to you, "not our department".

So moving on, what have we got? Islam – good. Anything else? Freedom. Yes, good. They don't like freedom. Very good. Islam and freedom-no-likey. We're building the picture. Ah – yes, Jolyon, interesting point about our chaps supporting this or that side out there in the desert. Do you follow horses, Jolyon? You see it's no use telling a betting man to stay away from the races, is it? That's what we do. We go in there and back winners and losers. One day your horse comes in, next time he runs he flops. That's what it's like out there. But either way, it's nothing to do with what we're talking about here. Even if it was, there's nothing we can do about it. It's another department. And just because some of the loot finds its way into these jonnies' hands is neither here nor there...

So, look, we've got to pull some threads together here – we've got to defend freedom – check. We've got to watch out for Islam – check. We've got to support Number 10 in what they do. We have to keep going out there, backing horses. OK, off you go and, mind the step on the way out.'

I sometimes fear...

I sometimes fear that people might think
that fascism arrives in fancy dress
worn by grotesques and monsters
as played out in endless re-runs of the Nazis.
Fascism arrives as your friend.
It will restore your honour,
make you feel proud, protect your house,
give you a job, clean up the neighbourhood,
remind you of how great you once were,
clear out the venal and the corrupt,
remove anything you feel is unlike you...
It doesn't walk in saying,
'Our programme means militias, mass imprisonments,
transportations, war and persecution.'

A short walk in Bologna

Lying next to a man playing a saxophone
is a dog with the face of a lion

On the ceiling above where we walk
is a head with three legs

In the square next to the fountain
is a golden man who doesn't move

In a shop selling bags
is a handbag in the shape of a butterfly

Next to the golden man in the square
is a balloon made into a flower

On the side of a long building
is a wall of photos
of people who fought to save this city

Amos the shepherd curses the rulers of ancient Israel

adapted from the Old Testament

Amos says:
'You have sent a whole people into exile;
you have forgotten how to be brothers to others.
In your fury,
you have lost all sense of pity.

You have sold innocent men for money;
you have crushed the poor and the needy;
you have taken their grain
so that you can build yourself fine stone houses.
You have even attacked pregnant women
so that you might make your country larger.

In your palaces you store up your own violence
just as you hoard your plunder and loot.
You lie on your marble couches,
stretch out on your beds,
eating the lambs of our flocks of sheep,
eating the calves from our herds of cattle,
drinking basinfuls of wine,
anointing yourselves with fine oils,
turning away the poor at your gate.

You dare to think that the instruments you sing to
are playing the music of David –
you who do not feel the pain and sorrow
of destroying the word of Joseph.

In time
you too will go into exile,
you will not even drink the wine
from the vineyards you've made;
and the great banquets you once feasted on
will slip into the past
just like your dreams of never-ending power.'

In Gaza

In Gaza, children,
you learn that the sky kills
and that houses hurt.
You learn that your blanket is smoke
and breakfast is dirt.

You learn that cars do somersaults
clothes turn red,
friends become statues,
bakers don't sell bread.

You learn that the night is a gun,
that toys burn
breath can stop,
it could be your turn.

You learn:
if they send you fire
they couldn't guess:
not just the soldier dies –
it's you and the rest.

Nowhere to run,
nowhere to go,
nowhere to hide
in the home you know.

You learn that death isn't life,
the air isn't bread.
The land is for all – you have the right to be
not dead.
The land is for all – you have the right to be
not dead.
The land is for all – you have the right to be
not dead.
The land is for all – you have the right to be
not dead.

Don't mention the children

'Israel bans radio advert listing names of children killed in Gaza.'
Guardian, 24 July 2014

Don't mention the children.
Don't name the dead children.
The people must not know the names
of the dead children.
The names of the children must be hidden.
The children must be nameless.
The children must leave this world
having no names.
No one must know the names of
the dead children.
No one must say the names of the
dead children.
No one must even think that the children
have names.
People must understand that it would be dangerous
to know the names of the children.
The people must be protected from
knowing the names of the children.
The names of the children could spread
like wildfire.
The people would not be safe if they knew
the names of the children.
Don't name the dead children.
Don't remember the dead children.
Don't think of the dead children.
Don't say: 'dead children'.

For the thousandth time

For the thousandth time
we have heard Israeli spokespeople tell us how
if you were living in London and getting rockets coming over
wouldn't you want to defend yourselves?
So we will reply that
if we are living in London and every way in and out
of London is guarded, checked and controlled by you,
every inch of airspace above us, every inch of sea-space next to us
is guarded, checked and controlled by you,
wouldn't we want to do things to stop you doing this to us?
And for doing this
we get massacred?

Who is the enemy?

Who is the enemy?
The enemy are the people who do terrible things.
Do we do terrible things?
No.
Who is our friend?
Our friends are good.
Do they do terrible things?
No.
Thank you, I am happy now.
Tra la... tra la.

What is racism?

This another way of telling the story I tell elsewhere in this book. I think of it as being more portable. Portable is important.

It's a clockmender who left his country to get a better living
and all is fine
until things start changing
there's an invasion
he and his wife run to another town
and the people who are supposed to keep law and order
decide to put him and his wife on a list
and then they decide that they will make them wear a special badge
marking them out as different
and then they decide that they will take all their money away from
them
and the clockmender and his wife have nothing much more they can
do
but sell old clothes in the market
where they must put a special badge on their stall marking them out
as different
and they send letters to America for help from their relatives
and they hear stories about how people like them are being shot
and transported to places where they never come back from
so they run again
and they hear rumours of a place where they'll be safe
and they get there somehow
and then someone from the army that invaded
arrives and he hates people like the clockmender
and his wife and he has lists
and with the help of the people
who are supposed to keep law and order
he gets hold of the clockmender and his wife
and he puts them on a train to a housing estate
which has been converted into a kind of prison
and from there they are shipped to a big station
and from there they are shipped out of the country

to a special place where people will work till they die
where people are tortured
where people starve to death
where people fall ill and have no means of being cured
where people are shot
where people are gassed to death
and the clockmender and his wife
are never seen again...
No one in their family knows what happened to them
for years and years
until one of the letters that the clockmender sent to America
turns up
and bit by bit one of the people in the family
finds the books that have the lists of the people
who like the clockmender were rounded up and shipped out
and bit by bit he puts the story together
he doesn't fully know why he's doing this
other than that he doesn't want it to be
that no one knows
he doesn't want it to be that people specialise
in saying that such things didn't happen
so he finds out more and more about the clockmender and his wife
and the clockmender is called Oscar, known as Jeschie
and his wife is Rachel
and Oscar is Oscar Rosen who was my father's uncle
and now you know
what I found out
now you know what I wanted you to know
and now I know
that this isn't something that
no one knows.

Then what?

So you say the land is yours.
Then what?
So you put hundreds of thousands to flight.
Then what?
So you take over land.
Then what?
So you round up thousands.
Then what?
So you build a wall.
Then what?
So you bulldoze homes.
Then what?
So you drop bombs.
Then what?
So you invade.
Then what?
So you kill children.
Then what?
So you shell hospitals.
Then what?
So you say you won't talk to terrorists.
Then what?
So you say the land is yours.
Then what?

Thanks

Just to clear something up,
we need mega rich people –
bankers and owners of giant corporations
otherwise there wouldn't be any work for anyone.
People wouldn't know how to do anything.
People would sit around all day, dying.
Luckily we have enormously rich people who,
out of the kindness of their hearts,
give us jobs to do.
That's why we can eat.
It's thanks to them.

Miliband, UKIP and the 'I'm not racist but...' people

Am fascinated
by these 'I'm not racist but' people they show us.
They say things like 'it's all got too much'
and 'there's too many of them' etc etc.
So what do they think UKIP is going to do for them?
Put people on trains and ship them out?
And how will these people be chosen?
And who is going to do the choosing?
And if the people refuse to go?
Will UKIP have special police to do that?
And this is not racism?
And UKIP isn't deliberately holding out hopes for people who
say those things that that is precisely what UKIP would do?
And Labour can't say that about UKIP?
And that Labour can't stop saying that 'people have concerns' instead
of saying what I'm saying here?
For f.sake Miliband, it's what your parents fled from.
Say it. Say it. Say it.

Anxious

Politicians keep telling me I'm anxious about immigration.
They say, people are anxious about immigration.

I'm not anxious about immigration.
I'm anxious about what power people think they can get
by saying that people are anxious about immigration.

Ban Santa

I propose:
For the sake of consistency
that those countries which ban the 'veil'
must, yes, must
ban the Santa outfit now.
It really is preposterous to allow these men
to cover up their faces in public places.
In our equal society,
it shows a complete disregard for equality,
because it gives Santas a sense of male superiority.
Think about it:
Only a man can be a Santa.
Ban the Santa Outfit Now.
News just in:
a child was in a Santa's grotto
and because of the Santa beard covering his face,
the child couldn't understand a word
of what the Santa was trying to say.
The child was upset by this and couldn't be consoled.
For how much longer are we going to have to tolerate
these people in our midst?
Ban the Santa Outfit now.
These Santas come here with their weird German-American ideas
about our traditional English Christmas,
with our traditional holly, ivy, yule log and Old King Cole
and our very own jolly old Father Christmas ho ho ho
and what do they do?
They give us German-American Santa Claus
with this ludicrous face-hiding garb,
muttering in strange unintelligible ways to our children.
Ban the Santa Outfit now.
I'm not racist but
I'm not racist but
I'm not racist but
I think there are limits to what we can tolerate

before our very own English spirit of toleration
is itself threatened.
How much longer before we see Santas on every street corner?
How much longer before we see Santas all the year round?
How much longer before we see young people wanting to
dress up as Santas?
Ban the Santa Outfit now.
Some of them are moderate Santas
They wear a small beard,
They keep their hoods down
They don't keep saying ho ho ho
every time you try to talk to them.
I'm not against them.
It's the full-bearded, hooded Santas we've got to look at
and ask ourselves what kind of society do we want?
Have we bent over too far in trying to be understanding?
Are we going to see a rash of Santas across Britain
jabbering away in their little grottos?
Ban the Santa outfit now.
And in the crazy PC world we live in
people think it's right and proper
to invite them into our schools
to talk to our children.
In years to come we might be seeing
fully hooded bearded Santas
in every classroom in the country.
People are saying to me when I meet them
that it feels like the invasion of an alien force.
Did we fight the Second World War
for our old traditional English department stores
to be invaded by these hooded men in red?
Their faces obscured, muttering
unintelligibly to our vulnerable children?
Time to take a stand:
Ban the Santa Outfit Now.

Caesar curbs immigrants in the year 0AD

Acting on behalf of Augustus Caesar, I would say that it's become clear to me that migrants from Galilee are bringing down the wages of those in Judea. On these grounds I am instructing the loyal king of Judea to stop all people at the border trying to enter Judea.

Meanwhile, it may be necessary to reduce the population as it has now been proved that high population causes poverty. The disturbances and riots that will almost certainly ensue will require us – that is, our client monarch, Herod – to reassert our power in the country by the usual means. At this moment in time, it will involve the termination of infant lives. Divisions between the peoples will enhance our rule.

We expect to appoint a Governor in the region soon after.

Nigel Farage reads *Lessons in Scapegoating* on the train

1. Identify a group of people as the 'other'. Do this by remarking on aspects of their life you can say are 'different' even though you or your family have those aspects too. Useful 'differences' may be such things as what language people speak, clothes they wear or how people stand in the street. Sporting allegiance is useful too. Don't worry about contradictions e.g. that your partner speaks another language, or that you stand about in the street too.

2. These 'other' people must be identified as causing a lowering of people's standards of living. It is vital that the people with real power in the country are not identified as lowering people's standards of living.

3. Indicate that these 'other' people can be and will be 'removed' in some way or another. Never indicate how they will be removed as past records on this matter are sensitive. When anyone says to you, 'Are you going to remove these "other" people?', deny it immediately. It doesn't matter either way – the point has been made. People will vote for you because they believe that you will 'get rid' of these 'other' people.

4. Never fill in any detail about how 'removal' of these 'other' people would affect the standard of living of those remaining. Just make vague mentions of 'work permits'. This gives the impression that 'other' people can be reduced to being a 'work permit' and that they can be cut off from partners, parents and children. They can just be hired and then 'sent back' somewhere.

5. It's vital to link such things as 'crime' to these 'other people' as if crime was invented by them. Any criminal activity on the part of people in your party or the 'people' (i.e. the not-other people) should be overlooked.

6. It's vital to suggest that the 'people' own the country and that it's been taken away from them by the 'other people'. The fact that the country is owned by a tiny, tiny group of extremely wealthy people should not be mentioned. The fact that this has always been the case should not be mentioned either. It's vital to keep the idea going that ordinary people 'own' the country and it's been 'taken away' from them by 'other' people who are not the tiny group of extremely wealthy people.

Wages

I keep hearing that immigrants cut wages.
So who's that sitting in the board room fixing the wage levels?
Immigrants?
Or employers?
Let's try that again, then..
Who cuts wages?
It's employers.

The deficit

A team from the TV rushed down to a food bank and
asked the people about the deficit. Could they think of
ways of bringing down the deficit?
No, it didn't seem as if they could.
We have hard choices to make, said the team, should
we cut hospitals or schools or social services? Or should
wages come down?
The people at the food bank said that they would prefer
it if it was none of those things.
You have to choose, said the TV team.
Why now? said one of the people. It wasn't as bad as
this a few years ago.
It's pretty complicated, said the TV team, but you remember
there was a banking crisis? As a result we've got to
get ourselves back in the black.
The thing is, said another one of the people, we haven't
got any money to do much about this deficit. Why not go and
ask the people with money?
Ah, no, said the TV team, that would be like pulling down
a building in order to keep it up.
Ah well, said one of the people in the line, if you're talking
about buildings, it's not money that actually builds the
buildings, is it?
Sorry, don't get you, said the people on the TV team, so
what's it to be, schools or hospitals?

Street clothes

I was watching a channel that I didn't know existed
and a man was explaining that they had been doing
visual research on street clothes and they had picked
up on the meme of the ragged dress. The ragged
dress, he said, spoke as much of absence as presence
and that modernity asks us to represent the binary.
There were some stills of people sleeping rough and
some moving footage of refugees resting. The man
pointed at the clothes and said that there were gaps,
'aporia' through which we see the body. The body he
explained is never 'innocent' but is always constructed
in time and space and whether we inflict damage on it,
or enclose it, or restrict its movements or eroticize it,
these are choices. The man then opened another file
and showed the designs he had made for 'The Ragged
Dress'. I was watching a channel that I didn't know
existed.

Hurrah

Hurrah for mortgages, say the zero-hour contract workers.
Hurrah for mortgages, say the zero-hour contract workers.

You want a house?
You want a mortgage?
You want to get on the first rung of the housing ladder?
You want to be part of the property-owning democracy?
Are you happy that this is what the government is doing for you?

Yes – hurrah for mortgages, say the zero-hour contract workers,
and thanks to you,
there are now many more of us
on zero-hour contracts.

Jolly good, they say back to the zero-hour contract workers,
thanks to you not having a mortgage
you won't be 'sub-prime'
you won't trigger a crash.

Hurrah for mortgages anyway, say the zero-hour contract workers
we love our property-owning democracy
even though we're not property-owning.
We love spending most of what we earn
so we can't save to buy our way into
the property-owning democracy.

And thank you, David Cameron
for telling us on the *Today* programme
of your 'thrill'
that day you walked through the door
of your first flat
knowing that it was yours.

Everyone on zero-hour contracts
cheered
when you said that...

Hurrah, hurrah, hurrah.

The bag

The doorbell rang and when I opened it there was a man there with a bag. He said that he was on a government scheme to take him off benefits which is why he was going to try to sell me stuff. He showed me an ID which had a picture of him next to a union jack. He was from Middlesbrough. He opened his bag and inside the bag were oven gloves, onion shredders, ironing board covers, computer screen cleaners, windscreen wiper renewal packs, pizza cutters, GCSE English revision books, passport form-filling guides, Protein-plus muscle bulking fluid, maps of Great Britain, Europe and Utopia, DIY botox kits, 3-1 on Arsenal winning the London derby, Job interview shirts, blood transfusions, heavenly choruses and lottery prizes. I bought the onion shredders.

Smart bombs

Thanks to our new rigorous testing procedures
some missiles and bombs have been designated as 'smart'.
All these armaments leave with a world class qualification
which show that they have reached a gold standard
level of attainment.
What happens after that is beyond our control.

It's not fully understood that Israeli shells, bullets and bombs
are more merciful than other people's shells, bullets and bombs.
Israel has selected the finest and greatest representatives
of Jewish thought and Jewish ideas and poured them
into the shells, bullets and bombs enabling them to produce
an especially spiritual and humanitarian killing.

Regeneration blues

Once upon a time
in days of old
great minds tried to figure
how to turn metal
into gold
They dreamed of the day
when a chunk of iron
could make them rich:
turn junk into treasure
a magic formula.

They failed.
Never found it.

But the news is: it's happened near you.
In the city centres
along by the canals
and the old railway yards
land worth a little
is now worth a lot.
The same patch of mud
sitting under a shed
under an old shop
car park or cinema
has turned into gold.

In the town halls
Councillors get excited:
'That old street
full of shops
run by people from
Africa, Turkey, the Middle East
with flats up above –
aren't they on short lease
'cos we were once

going to put a road through there?
That old pool
that old school,
don't we own that?
You know what?
We could demolish the lot.
Get developers in:
no time to wait,
Reeee – generate.

Modernise
Energise
Put up high-rise.

Buy to rent
For young professionals
Yo-pros, don't you know.
Change the geography
Change the demography...'

So the developers arrive
with their brochures
and sharp shoes
their power points
and bullet points.

They've done the sums
They can make it work
If the council plays a part:
If it compensates
Decontaminates
Covers losses
Shares the load
Builds a road
It's a partnership
Public private
Private public
The area will be
privatised.

Our money will
subsidi-i—ize.
The deal is done.

But the law says 'Consult'
A meeting is held
and on the screen are:
the derelict sheds
and the crumbling shops
'Look!' they say, 'the area will die.
We'll build towers of steel and glass
to the sky.'

Towers full of the salaried and sleek
Towers with no old people or babies
Towers for people who need gifts and coffee
only available from brand-name shops.

'Transport links will improve,'
say the Councillors we elect.
'Everyone will benefit, don't object.
There'll be a new library.
in there...
somewhere.'

The meeting is noisy.
The shopkeepers say,
the tenants say
they want to stay.

People say
They want the Turkish bread
and the Indian rice.
Someone says that the buildings are old
they could be restored.
Why take away memories?
They used to make places
where we could walk about:
squares and cul-de-sacs,
not canyons between tower blocks.

Someone says,
We're desperate for places where families can live,
places where kids can play
clinics on hand, not miles away
and ground floor flats for the old and disabled.

The meeting ends in a riot
when one of the Councillors
says: 'People round here have no ambition
They want to live in a dump
and the people in it
are the dregs on drugs.'

It goes to committee
and five men sit and take a vote.
It goes 2 votes to 2
Even stevens
So the chair says he must decide.
He's in favour of high-rise
A great leap forward for the community
A revolution in thinking, a retail opportunity.

Within a week the bulldozers hit
the shopkeepers and tenants have to quit.

Someone digs in files and papers
and finds that the chairman of the committee
is on the board of a firm
that will supply the locks
in the high-rise blocks.

But it's too late to stop.
He says he forgot
to declare an interest.
But it's too late to stop.

History doesn't matter
The people who live there don't matter
The people who run shops don't matter
People who need places for people who have kids
don't matter
Nurseries, clinics, opens spaces, good cheap housing,
don't matter.

'Look', say the Councillors
'It's Regeneration!'
And they don't mean
Regeneration
of the developers' bank accounts.

As the blocks go up
it's income up.
But it's us who subsidize
private high-rise.
Regeneration is a lie
Regeneration is a lie
Regeneration is
Degeneration
Regeneration
Is degeneration.

Conversations

When I was at university I used to come home
and late evening I'd get into long conversations
with my father. Sometimes these would last
until two or three in the morning until my mum
would bang on the floor and tell us to get to bed.
I remember one time he said that it was down to
us to change the world now. He and his friends
had tried and had made mistakes.

'How's it going?' he said.

I said we were doing our best. We have
meetings.

'And?' he said.

I said that the meetings were really good and we
weren't going to make the same mistakes. He
asked me what was it like where I was living and
I said that there were was a gang of us in a house.

'All students?' he said.

'No, there's a whole load of us who had met
up in the meetings, but there's also a guy who
works on the sites. He's a gas. He gets dressed up
in his site gear and goes to bed in it. Boots an' all.
Then in the morning, his alarm rings and he steps
straight out of bed, out the room, down the stairs
and out the house.'

Mum banged on the floor. My dad got up. On the
way out he said, 'Put the bit about changing the
world on hold.'

'Oh no,' I said, 'this time it's going to happen.'

'No,' he said, 'not till you do something about him
going to work in his sleep.'

'No,' I said, 'you don't get it. He's having a laugh.
We're getting there.'

'Switch the fire off when you turn in,' he said.

The same

When I was at school, we were all the same.
Except – we weren't. I mean there were kids
whose parents came from Ireland but they
kept their heads down and pretended that
they hadn't come from a place like Ireland.
There were kids whose parents came from
Scotland and Wales. That was more OK.
Sometimes a kid came in from America or
Germany or Poland. You could pick them out
from the colour of their shoes. And then there
were the Chinese sisters. And the Jews. Were we
the same? Same as what? We weren't even
the same as each other. One of us had parents
who came over from Germany. Others it was
mostly grandparents or great-grandparents
from Poland and Russia. For some of the Jews,
the big thing was jazz and blues: Charlie Parker,
Miles Davis. Some it was Ban the Bomb. Some it
was Toulouse-Lautrec and Van Gogh. Some it was
not eating bacon. There was a day when some
people in the USA said that it was going to the
End of the World. So some of us said that we
would hold a ceremony on the school field to
bring in the End of the World. We turned our
jackets inside out and wore them that way. Soon
the field was full of hundreds of us. Looked like
most of the school was there. The head and
deputy heads rushed out and said that it
had to stop. I think they thought that there was
going to be an uprising.

Do not ask

*'Undercover police spied on grieving families
of de Menezes, Groce and Reel'
Guardian,* 24 July 2014

If you are a person of colour
if the police think you are a person of colour
if the police think that you might be a person of colour
if one of your family is killed
if one of your family is killed by the police
you should assume that the police
will dress up in plain clothes
and hide amongst people you know
and watch what you do
while you grieve for the person who was killed
you should assume that they will make notes
about you and your family
and that they will keep these notes for as long as they can.
If you wonder why or how this keeps you safe
if you wonder why or how this keeps the rest of us safe
do not ask the police why they made notes about you
do not ask the police why they kept these notes about you,
and if you are not one of the people who is from a family
with a member who was killed
but you are curious
as to why the police would do these things
do not ask why or how any of this happens
because the police will keep notes about you too.

Tory UK

The Tory UK is a low wage UK, low benefits UK, low tax UK, small welfare state UK, big profits UK.

The Tory UK is more people working for less money UK. A few super-rich people making more money and paying less tax UK.

The Tory UK is having less chance of the state being able to look after you in times of need UK.

All this is what he means by a 'strong' economy UK.

Gottit, Dave UK.

Looking for someone to head the enquiry...

They'll be scouring the country for another peer
who they can pretend is uncontaminated
hoping that people betrayed and humiliated
will be cowed and passive before power,
will accept the assurances of grandees
schooled since birth in the art of domination.

Panic is spreading. For one brief moment
the suits and robes look tattered,
the velvet curtain has parted, we have sight
of the cogs and wheels which hold our rulers
aloft, seemingly forever triumphant.

Before it closes and they reappear glossed
and strident, let's hold that picture in our heads
for when they order us to have less
while they take more, when they take what's ours
and give to those who already have.

They are only what they are: people pumped up
by pumped-up people; people paraded before us
as wiser or cleverer or worthier than us.

They are none of these things. They are just people
who hope that we are too tired or too afraid to
get rid of them.

NHS

These are the hands
That touch us first
Feel your head
Find your pulse
And make your bed.

These are the hands
That tap your back
Test the skin
Hold your arm
Wheel the bin.

These are the hands
That change the bulb
Fix the drip
Pour the jug
Replace your hip.

These are the hands
That fill the bath
Mop the floor
Flick the switch
Soothe the sore.

These are the hands
That burn the swabs
Give us a jab
Throw out sharps
Design the lab.

And these are the hands
That stop the leaks
Empty the pan
Wipe the pipes
Carry the can.

These are the hands
That clamp the veins
Make the cast
Log the dose
And touch us last.

The wars must go on...

How was it when you planned the first gulf war and the second and the war in Afghanistan and the war in Libya? Did you sit in your bunkers and convince yourselves that these were wars which would only be fought where you were dropping bombs? Did you imagine that every time an unarmed civilian died that this would be forgotten? Did you imagine that every act of killing you took, was to defend us? Did anyone in the bunker hold up his hand and say, 'Perhaps I should just raise the possibility that people in the world, who have links to the places we are bombing, will think that they can join the war, by fighting it in our countries over here...' Was he shouted down? Was he told that he was a wishy-washy liberal, someone soft on multiculturalism, a relativist, a false witness, or what? Was he told that he was a fool and didn't understand that these wars are wars of known consequences and all these consequences are good ones: peace, democracy, liberal values? These are wars to end wars. And he, the foolish man, couldn't see that these were wars which would advance civilisation? And if at any point in the future anyone were to raise the possibility that attacks might be made on liberal western countries in response to these wars, the foolish man would be told that there was no linkage, no unforeseen consequences. The war must go on. The wars must go on. And on. Civilisation is just round the corner. One last push. One last drone. One last bomb. One last invasion. C'mon!

The economy

The 'economy'... how we love to hear that the economy is doing well, the economy is picking up, there's a strong economy. When we hear that, we know that things are looking good. Things are getting better. The economy. How we love the economy when it's doing well. If fact, we can be doing very badly when the economy is doing well. That doesn't matter, though. If we know the economy is doing well, we feel good. In fact, many hundreds of thousands of people may be doing very badly, and still the economy might be doing well. How mysterious. How could that be? Could it be that the economy is doing well precisely because hundreds of thousands of people are doing badly? Could it be that when people are paid less or hardly anything at all, this makes it easier for very few people to make much more? Could it be that what goes for the 'economy' is really a way of talking about how successful those people are at doing well out of paying people less or hardly anything at all? Yes, an economy can be doing well, with people begging in the street. Never mind that, though. The economy is doing well. We love to hear that. Even the beggars love to hear that. They can't afford a radio or TV so you'll have to tell them. Why not pop down to a job centre near you and say, 'Hello everyone, the economy is doing well, the economy is strong'? They'll love it.

Normality

Here's how normality works.

On the *Today* programme we heard a woman from the NHS say:
'...the financial constraints we're under in this country'.
Then later we heard an item how 'Apple put their profits in a tax haven...'
(In fact they borrow money against these profits
– presumably at a very low interest rate –
and buy bonds in their own company
– presumably offsetting it all against tax...
Search me, I don't fully figure that bit of the fiddle,
but it 'saves' them millions, and takes it away from tax take in US, UK etc etc...)
If Apple are doing it, then so are others...
'Financial constraints...' – me arse.

Two thoughts

1

This government have perfected a new collective art form: blaming the poor for being poor and blaming professionals for deliberately keeping them in poverty. Boris says professionals are stupid; Gove blames teachers; IDS blames benefits; Cameron blames immigrants etc etc. The one group whose fault it can't be are those who become extremely wealthy from employing people on low wages.

2

The continuation of the system turns on how successful our leaders can be in keeping up the illusion that everyone or anyone can become rich. To do this, they have to point at the tiny minority of people who have done this and to ignore a) the fact that most wealth is retained dynastically by rich families and b) that the system works by virtue of there being a tiny minority who are rich and a massive majority who are not. So really the system is much more interested in guaranteeing that there are enough poor people doing the work than digging out the odd poor person who might possibly one day become rich. But that should remain a secret. Or at least not very well known. One way for that to happen is to tell everyone that life's a competition, work's a competition, your home is in a competition, love is a competition, your body is in a competition, you're in a competition with yourself and half of you is losing and the other half of you might become Alan Sugar, so keep working very hard for very little... for someone rather like Alan Sugar.

Wealth

If the things we find useful and enjoy and consume, don't come from human effort, where do they come from?

If the wealth that people make (when we come together to make and distribute the things we find useful, enjoy and consume), doesn't come from human effort, where does it come from?

If the people who take the unequal share of wealth (that comes when people run the outfits that do this) don't get it from taking an unequal share, where do they get it from?

Pressure on services

I keep hearing that immigrants put pressure on services.
For the past four years, we've had government ministers explaining why and how it's their job to put pressure on services. They call it cutting the deficit. They're proud of it. We call it, 'cutting services'. They have to do this because the international financiers say that it must be done.
So it's not immigrants putting pressure on services.
It's international financiers.
Funny that they don't say that.

David Whelan, money and Jews

Dave Whelan (owner of Wigan Football Club)
who says that Jews chase money more than anyone else
should be asked if he chases money.

If he doesn't, he must be the first football club owner in history not to.
If he does chase money, what's he complaining about?

The megaphone explains

The megaphone said:

The deficit is a terrible problem.
The deficit is terrible.
The deficit must stop.

We know how the deficit must stop:
Poor people have got too much money.
Poor people have too many hospitals.
Poor people have too many schools.
Poor people are getting too much help.

The good news is:
We are going to stop poor people being so greedy.
We are going to stop poor people earning so much.
We are going to stop poor people having so many hospitals.
We are going to stop poor people have so many schools.
We are going to stop poor people getting help.

The good news is:
This is going to make the economy healthy.
The good news is:
It's working.
How do we know it's working?
Because poor people are getting poorer.
and super-rich people are getting richer.

Please join me with celebrating this.
Hip hip hurrah
hip hip hurrah
hip hip hurrah

Magna Carta

When my mother was born
her mother didn't have the vote.
Women under 30 with no property
weren't ready to vote in 1919.
That's why my mother's mother would
wake up every morning
and say to herself,
'Thank God for the Magna Carta.'
She didn't know that
700 years earlier
all the women in England
and all the serfs
used to wake up every morning
and say,
'Thank God for the Magna Carta' too,
because they weren't in the Magna Carta either.

The conjuror

...and the conjuror appeared
and said,
'Ladies and Gentlemen, the art of conjuring
is to make things change before your very eyes
without you knowing how or why.
We show you things and in a flash
they disappear and reappear somewhere else
or reappear as something else altogether different.
Ladies and Gentlemen, watch closely, see
the fingers never leave the hand,
I want you to tell me what I have here:
Yes, it's a banking crisis, a full-blooded
international banking crisis, thank you.
Now, watch closely, don't take your eyes off it
and with no more than a moment of patter,
look again and what do I have?
A crisis in government spending.
That, Ladies and Gentlemen
is what conjuring is all about.
Thank you very much.'

The conjuror returns

'...Ladies and Gentlemen
let me show you something else.
You know and I know that conjuring
is often about distraction.
We entice you to watch one thing
while we are doing something else altogether.
So if I say, I would like you to keep your eyes
on what I've got here, you're going to be
suspicious, aren't you?
Well, I'll try it all the same.
It's a deficit. I want you to watch the deficit.
I am going to do all I possibly can to make
it disappear.
Now to do this I'm going to have to
move some money around over here.
Some people have a lot.
Some people have hardly any.
Will I be able to change that?
So, now you're confused.
Are you watching the deficit
or are you watching the money?
Remember, if I don't make the deficit disappear
I will have failed.
It's getting a bit smaller...
I promised I would...
but, Ladies and Gentlemen
it would be true to say
I haven't made it disappear.
Oh dear...
But Ladies and Gentlemen
what if that was all a ploy?
While you were watching the deficit
hoping to catch me out,
look what I did with the money over here.
I took money from those with hardly any

and gave it to those who have a lot.
And you didn't notice,
because you were watching the deficit.
Well, Ladies and Gentlemen
I may not have made the deficit disappear
but I certainly moved the money.
I call that a success.
What do you think?
Thank you very much.
You've been a lovely audience.'

Statement from the not-national union of non-doms

Those of us in the NNUND
utterly condemn the vicious and greedy threat
issued by the Labour Party, a threat that
will endanger our living standards.
We wish to express our solidarity with
the brave leadership of the Conservative Party
who have done all they can to maintain
our standard of living throughout these
difficult times. We would also like to thank
the *Daily Mail*, a paper owned by one of our
members who continue to highlight our hardship.

Great big bogeymen

Once upon a time, there was a great big bogeyman.
It was called 'Balance of Payments'
and everyone made a fuss about it.
Then 'Balance of Payments' disappeared.
Another time there was another great big bogeyman.
It was called 'Devaluation' and everyone made a fuss about it.
Then 'Devaluation' disappeared.
Another time there was another great big bogeyman.
It was called 'Productivity'.
Everyone made a fuss about it, then 'Productivity' disappeared.
There have been other bogeymen, like
'Money Supply'
but because they've all disappeared now
I don't remember what they were.
Now we have 'the Deficit'.
That's a very big bogeyman.
Everyone makes a fuss about it.
It's got to 'come down', everyone says.
Our newspapers and politicians love these great big bogeymen.
At the end of the day, making a fuss about
all these different bogeymen does the same thing:
it says to people that they should have lower wages.
Hurrah for great big bogeymen.
Maybe we'll have a new one soon.

Gods

I love the way in which commentators and experts
say the words 'the city' and 'the markets'.
They aren't given to us as groups of people
carrying out actions based on people's self-interest
or their desire to finish the day richer than they were
the day before.
They are talked of as elements in nature,
like the wind or mountains, yet mysteriously
and magically endowed with the power of manipulating
and determining our standard of living,
how much food we eat or what kind of home
or hospital or school we're allowed to have.
'The city' and 'the markets', we're told, are 'uneasy'
about us having too much.
And commentators invite us to think that
that's because some law of nature has been broken.
'The city' and 'the markets' are like the gods
in ancient Greece, like Poseidon who was
enraged when Odysseus maimed his son,
and went on taking revenge for years after.
Yet 'the city' and 'the markets' are just people
who do things like sell each other debts so big
they'll never be paid back
or buy promises and guesses that can never
materialise.
And they don't stop doing what they're doing
even as the great towers and offices they work in
have to close
and thousands lose their jobs.
These are our gods.

Thieves: taxmen or someone else?

Bloke tells me that taxmen are 'thieves'.

Hang on, pal.
Every minute that the workforce works,
the pay they receive is only a percentage
of the total value of all goods or services
that are outputted.
So, yes, some of what's left goes on investment,
marketing, rent, and buying materials.
What's left after that is profit.
This profit produces the rich and the super-rich.
The super-rich are getting richer by the day.
The workforce is either staying the same or
going backwards.
Now, let's talk about 'thieves' again...

Both rich and poor took a hit

When someone stands in front of you and
claims that both rich and poor took a hit
following the great bankers' crash of 2008
you know that you're dealing with someone
who thinks that buying a Merc
instead of a Rolls
is the same as buying economy crisps
instead of meat.

From Labour deficit till now in seven steps

1. Under Labour, there was a deficit of £36 billion or so. None of our leaders on either side of electoral politics said it was a problem.
2. There was a worldwide banking and finance crisis.
3. The deficit shot up.
4. The Tories cooked up the idea that this high deficit was caused by Labour's deficit and not by the banking crisis. Not even Mervyn King ex-boss of the Bank of England believes this.
5. The Tories cooked up the idea that the way to bring this high deficit down was to cut wages, cut welfare, cut public services.
6. When that didn't work, they've spent some more government money and printed £350 billion. That has hardly worked either.
7. The super-rich have got super-richer, the poor have got poorer, a lot of people in between have stood still or lost in real terms against prices.
8. Some of us think that has been the real aim of deficit-talk and austerity anyway.

Grant Shapps

Grant Shapps
is several chaps.
People in the
media
think he fiddled wikipedia.
Grant Shapps
never lies.
He mistakenly
over firmly denies.

Dear William Shakespeare,
on your anniversary

450 years to the good, do we see
In celebration thereof, have I offerings for thee.

Insults have I plucked from thy poems and plays
For use by tweeters, in these digital days.

Thou cream faced loon
There's no more faith in thee than in a stewed prune
Thou art baser than a cutpurse.
We know each other well. We do, and long to know each other worse.
Thou thing of no bowels thou. Pied ninny! Scurvy patch!
Thou clay-brained guts, thou knotty-pated fool,
Thou whoreson obscene greasy tallow-catch.
Thou poisonous slave,
filthy worsted-stocking knave.
Damn'd and luxurious mountain-goat.
The gold I give thee will I melt and pour down thy ill-uttering throat.
Thou art nothing better than a disease.
His breath stinks with toasted cheese.
Slanderous tongues,
the food is such as hath been belched on by infected lungs
Braggart vile
thy tongue outvenoms all the worms of Nile
O you beast, o faithless coward, o dishonest wretch,
wilt thou be made a man out of my vice?
It is certain that when he makes water, his urine is congealed ice.

Go rot
Get thee glass eyes; and, like a scurvy politician,
Seem to see the things, thou dost not.

William's works will live on where'er he doth rove
In spite of, methinks, not because of Mr Gove.

NormCheck

Here at NormCheck, we are looking closely at the principles of exam marking. We regret that many people are under the mistaken impression that exams serve the purpose of enabling individuals to amass a specific amount of knowledge in an important field relevant to what will be that person's life beyond and after the exam. We work very hard to eliminate as much 'usefulness' from the exam system as we can. We are also extremely vigilant in eliminating what progressives have called 'transferrable skills'. In the world outside the classroom, it may well be the case that people's ability to interpret data in unexpected ways, to invent new ways of doing things, to know how to investigate something unfamiliar, to co-operate with colleagues and strangers – are all useful but that's of no concern of ours. At NormCheck we are putting a great deal of effort into ensuring that education – that's to say exams – are solely concerned with core facts. Luckily, at the Department for Instruction, we have people who know what these core facts are. They have all studied either PPE at Oxford, pure economics or law – and, thankfully, all had some experience of a private education.

So, to recap, the exams themselves are not for the purpose of the individual to acquire and retain anything useful. They are solely for the purpose of us to grade, select and segregate people. This is why exams aren't tests of what people know on a given day. They are a means by which we can draw a line across a group of people and say, all of you above that line are a success, all of you below that line are a fail. What we do at NormCheck is move the line. That's our job. Each year, we meet up, have an extremely nice lunch and spend the afternoon working out where we'll put the line. This has nothing whatsoever to do with whether this or that pupil knows anything or not. It is entirely to do with where we decide to put the line. This depends on such things as what the Secretary of State at the Department for Instruction thinks, which itself is usually dependent on what the editor of the *Daily Mail* thinks.

Exams

A lot of time is being wasted in schools trying to teach a whole lot of unnecessary stuff. The point of schools is to pass exams. Exams are tests in who can write fast. Or put another way, exams find out who can write slowly. That's what they're for. So, instead of wasting loads of time muddling this up with writing answers to questions that no one cares about, schools can concentrate on the business of learning to write fast. And of course, it's not just about writing fast. It's about writing fast for over an hour. In hard exams it can be for two hours. And when I say 'writing' this has to be writing by hand. This is really important. I'm out and about in the real world, and all the successful people I meet spend several hours every day writing fast by hand. So my school of the future will be full of children writing fast by hand. And, here's the innovation: they won't be thinking at the same time. To be really fast, they'll be copying. In front of them will be iPads or laptops, with a lot of writing up on screen. It can be anything, ads for soft drinks, poems that celebrate a well-known fast food, instructions for self-assembly wardrobes... and the children will be copying these. Teachers – or teaching assistants, or assistants to teaching assistants can come round and if a child is slowing down, they can give them a little nudge to remind them to speed up.

Then at the end of the year, when the child's fate is to be decided, the big exam will discover who can really write fast, who can write not-so-fast, who writes slowly and who writes really, really slowly.

Guide to education

You get education in schools.
To find out how much education you get,
the government gives you tests.
Before you do the tests
the government likes it if you are put on
different tables that show how well or badly
you are going to do in the tests.
The tests test whether they
have put you on the right table.
The tests also test whether you know what you're
supposed to know.
But
don't try to get to know any old stuff like
'What is earwax?' or 'how to make soup'.
The way to know things you're supposed to know
is to do pretend tests.
When you do the pretend tests
you learn how to think in the way that tests
want you to think.
The more practice you do,
the more likely it is that you won't make the mistake
of thinking in any other way other than in
the special test way of thinking.
Here's an example:
The apples are growing on the tree.
What is growing on the tree?
If you say, 'leaves', you are wrong.
It's no use you thinking that when apples are on a tree
there are usually leaves on the tree too.
There is only one answer. And that is 'apples'.
All other answers are wrong.
If you are the kind of person that thinks 'leaves' is a
good answer, doing lots and lots and lots of practice tests
will get you to stop thinking that 'leaves' is a good answer.
Doing many, many practice tests will also make it

very likely that there won't be time for you to go out
and have a look at an apple tree to see what else
grows on apple trees. Like ants. Or mistletoe.
Education is getting much better these days
because there is much more testing.
Remember, it's 'apples' not 'leaves'.

Examz Inc

Here at Examz Inc., we've been doing some blue sky thinking about Projectile Vomiting (PV). Here's the definition: 'vomiting that is sudden and so vigorous that the vomit is forcefully projected to a distance'. We've commissioned an extensive study on the application of PV principles in the assessment field. First reports suggest that we have a lot to learn from this important work. In PV, it's essentially a matter of WAGICSO – what goes in, comes straight out. It's the most efficient system known to man of the 'return' principle. Almost nothing is wasted. Our researchers applied this principle to fact-consumption and fact-delivery.

What would be the most efficient PV replication in the education field? It turns out that for many years we've been nearly there, but not there. Schools and exam boards have been content with what in the field of physiology would be, say, spitting out, dribbling and slow vomiting. In all these cases, there is a lack of efficiency: slow return, inefficient delivery – and more importantly – a persistent danger of residue,: small amounts remain inside the person.

If we apply PV to the education situation, we bolt teaching to instruction and not waste time with any activity that might obstruct PV-type delivery. So, quite clearly, the best known system of PV delivery in the assessment field are lengthy exams in which there are only right and wrong answers and uncomfortable seating arrangements.

Preparation for PV delivery exams should consist of PV delivery practice, once a week. For four days of the week, the instructor instructs with the PV material, that is to say, the consumption side. Day five is PV day, with all-day instruction on how to eliminate repetition, hesitation, deviation, discussion, co-operation, investigation, invention, interpretation or compassion, followed by a two hour PV exam. Research suggests that when PV is applied, it is the most efficient way of guaranteeing that pupils retain as little as possible of what they have consumed. This is part of the new Empowerment Agenda much favoured by the new Department for Instruction, who argue that PV style learning is the world's most proven method of enabling disadvantaged children to fail exams.

How to run an education system

Send inspectors into schools.
Inspectors talk to the headteacher.
Inspectors say:
'We found a child who doesn't know his 12 x table.
Therefore your school "needs improvement".
Therefore we're making it an academy.
We have no evidence that making a school into an academy will help that child, but we'll do it anyway.'

'Tell them they're better off'

The King summoned his Great Adviser and said to him, 'Listen, the people are saying that they can't feed themselves, they can't buy what they need.'

The Great Adviser said, 'Tell them that they're better off.'

'But they won't believe me,' said the King.

'Some will believe you, some will think that you mean things will be better next year, and some will just become sullen.'

'Sullen?' said the King, 'will that be alright?'

'Of course it will,' said the Great Adviser, 'sullen means that they will just feel bad, say very little or blame the man next door.'

'Sounds good,' said the King.

'Off you go then,' said the Great Adviser, 'spread the good news.'

'I will,' said the King, 'but hang on a minute. What about the ones who will protest and say that we're lying?'

'With a bit of luck, there won't be enough of them to cause a problem,' said the Great Adviser, 'but if it starts to look difficult for us, I'll think of something else.'

History of humankind

It all started off with some monkeys
who were fed up with being monkeys.
Some of them said they wanted to be gorillas
but the others said, let's be humans,
except they couldn't say that yet;
they just did lots of living.

The humans lived in caves and painted
pictures of bison, they dressed up as bison,
they ate bison.

Then someone said let's plant seeds.
That was an alpha male who said that,
and he's been trying to plant his seeds
ever since.

A priest arrived and said, let us pray.
So everyone prayed.
The sun was really pleased and
because they prayed it turned up the next day too.

One day someone invented a wheel.
It went round.
Someone said, if we had four of them
and petrol we could make a car.
Not yet, someone said.

Aristotle turned up and figured out
how we think.
He also dissected a fish.

From then till now, people
loved being slaves or serfs.
This is brilliant, they said,
we love working for nothing
then dying.

Every now and then
there were revolts.
People said, sod this for a game of soldiers.
But it was risky because there were
kings, emperors, Caesars,
warlords, big chiefs.

Bad kings killed people and went broke.
Good kings killed people and were less broke.

People went on working
but we don't know their names.
Eventually they all went to work in factories.

For ages there was a load of trouble
to do with voting.
The people with names said voting was a bad idea.
The people with no names thought
it was a good idea because it would change things.
It didn't.
Now the people with names think it's a good idea.

Another big change was mass communication.
That's where people with names communicate
to the masses.
It's free because it's owned by free millionaires.

Two horrible men turned up
they both had moustaches.
In the end this has turned out well
because the people with names
have said that we're all lucky
that the men with moustaches aren't around anymore.

The way it works now is that
there is a small group of people who own
nearly everything.
The rest of us owe them money.

There's also *X-Factor*.

Music

There's a road near to where I live where
men sit in cars listening to music. I walk
past them trying to figure out if there's any
kind of link between the men. They don't listen
to the same kind of music. They're not the
same age. Their cars aren't the same. They
come to the same street. They sit in cars.
They listen to music. They drive off. I know
that they listen to music because it's loud
enough to hear outside the car. Sometimes
it's radio: Capital, Heart, Kiss, Radio 1,
Radio 2, Radio 3, Classic FM, Jazz Fm and
radio stations I don't know. Some days it's
music I want to hear. I stop and listen. They
don't seem to mind. They don't get out and
say, 'Stop listening to my music.' I don't think
I've ever seen one of them ever get out. Not
even that thing you have to do when you
sit in a car for a long time, open the door, get
out, shake your legs about and get back in.
They never do that. I don't know how long
they stay. I walked past one of them once
and it must have been loud enough for the
people in the house to hear. It was very early.
You would wake up and hear that in your
bedroom. You would want to come down
and knock on the car window and say:
'Excuse me, I was asleep.'
But then, he would just say, 'You're not
asleep now, though.'
Or you could come down and say,
'Excuse me, have you got any Tamla Motown?'
And I bet he would say, 'No.'
One night there was an old man doing it.
Very, very old with a white beard. I didn't

recognise the music. I'm guessing but it could have come from Turkey. He was smiling. That's another thing. They don't usually smile. This one was smiling. He was still there in the morning. The music was on. He was asleep. I think he was asleep. No way of knowing for certain.

The Noise

We were indoors when we heard a noise.
My flatmate said, 'Can you hear that?'
I said, 'What?'
He said, 'Listen.'
I said, 'I am listening.'
'No,' he said, 'shuttup and then you'll hear it.'
I stood absolutely still.
'I can hear you breathing,' I said.
'No, not that, 'he said, 'that.'
'That's the point,' I said, 'every time you say, "that" I
don't know the "that" you mean.'
'There,' he said.
'Just because you change the "that" to "there" doesn't
make it any easier.'
'That,' he said.
'Ah, you've switched back.' I said.
'Listen,' he said.
'Aeroplane,' I said.
'That's not an aeroplane,' he said.
An aeroplane passed overhead.
'That's an aeroplane,' I said.
'I know that's an aeroplane,' he said, 'I meant the noise.'
'The aeroplane is making a noise,' I said.
'I don't mean the aeroplane noise,' he said.
I listened really hard.
'Do you think it's an animal?' I said.
'I think it's industrial,' he said.
'There's no industry left round here,' I said.
'It's something with an industrial sound,' he said.
'Animals can make industrial sounds,' I said, 'the cats
make a kind of dvvvvvv sound sometimes when they're
sleeping.'
'There!' he said.
'That's someone's fridge,' I said.
'No one's fridge is that loud,' he said.

'Wrong,' I said, 'people are buying ancient fridges these days,
Some of them make that noise.'

'How ancient?'

'I don't know, fridges from the 1950s. I've seen them,' I said.

'It's a drill,' he said.

'Or a sander,' I said.

'Who would be sanding at this time?'

'Or a cement mixer.'

'Yes, it does sound like a cement mixer,' he said.

'No I meant, "who would be using a cement mixer at this
time?"' I said.

'But it does really sound like a cement mixer,' he said.

'There goes another aeroplane,' I said.

Radio

When I'm on my own I like to leave the radio on in
another room. I keep it at a level where I can't hear
the words, just the sound of words. The other day
I was busy thinking, but the radio was putting me off. I
went in to the room in order to switch it off. In the
room there was a woman interviewing a man. The
man was lying on the floor. She was asking him if he
saw the car. 'Did you see the car?' she said.
He said, 'I'm not on benefits.'
She said, 'I'm not asking you that. I'm trying to find out
about the incidence of accidents.'
I said, 'I'm trying to find out about the incidence of
incidents.'
She said, 'This is an accident black spot.'
I got in very quickly: *'Treasure Island!'*
The man lying on the floor said, 'The Black Spot!
That's it. It's all over.'
She said, 'I don't think it's as bad as that, you're
just a bit shaken up.'
'Robert Louis Stevenson!' I said very quickly.
She looked at me.
I said, 'The 'Louis' is pronounced 'Lewis' but spelt
L.O.U.I.S. Lewis. Though when you say it quickly you
don't know. It could be Louis or Lewis.
RobertLouisStevenson. Like that. On its own, though,
you could tell. Lewis. But spelt, L.O.U.I.S.'
We spent a few minutes practising saying
'RobertLouisStevenson.'

Once

Once there was a boy who
wanted to be beautiful
and a girl who
wanted to be strong.
The boy was worried
that he wasn't beautiful enough.
The girl was worried
that she wasn't strong enough.

One day they went out to seek
their fortunes.

But there was nothing.

There was nowhere for them to go
nothing for them to see
no one for them to meet.
There was no story for them
to be in.
Not even this one.

Tattoos

I had a thought that I would be the last person
in London who didn't have a tattoo. I was looking
in the window of a tattooing place and saw a sign
that said, 'Tattoos: seen, unseen and foreseen'.
I went in and said to the man, 'Excuse me but
your sign, "Tattoos: seen, foreseen, and unseen"
what's that about?'
He said, 'A tattoo that's seen is one that you can
see. A tattoo that's foreseen is one where you choose
which people you want to see it. A tattoo that's
unseen is one you can't see.'
'I get the "seen" tattoos,' I said, 'but what's this
foreseen one, how does that work?'
'They're digitally pre-arranged tattoos, so they
can only be seen by the people you choose.'
'Wow,' I said.
'There's an app on phones now,' he said, 'which we
hook up to. The app does it. You programme in
who you want to see your tattoo. I've got a tattoo
here,' he said pointing to his arm, 'now you can't
see a tattoo there, but now look on this phone,
and there – see – a tattoo.'
'Well, actually, I can't.'
'Oh, well, it's just booting up... but you will,' he said.
'Great,' I said, 'I can think of a lot of uses for that.
Now, the other one, unseen tattoo, is that one that's
hidden, like – under your clothes or something?'
'No,' he said, 'it's one that no one can see.'
'You mean, it's somewhere private?' I said
'No, no, it's an invisible tattoo,' he said, 'we do
the tattoo, anywhere on the client, but no one can
see it. I've got one here,' he said and pointed to
his arm. 'See that,' he said, 'you can't see that
can you?'
'No,' I said, 'that's perfect. I can't see a thing.'

Pizza

We ordered in a pizza and when it came
we talked about how we'd divvy it up.
He said that because I didn't eat as much
as him, I should have less. I said OK but
it wasn't much less than him and after all
it was me who had bought the pizza. He said
that was besides the point. This was about
eating not paying.
I said, 'Is it?'
So he said, 'How about thinking in eighths?'
I said, 'Go on, I can run with that.'
He said, 'How does five eighths and three
eighths sound to you?'
I said that I thought I was hungrier than three
eighths, and he said but 'hungrier' would be
four-eighths.
I said, 'What's wrong with that?'
And he said, 'Four eighths is the same as a half.'
I said, 'Is it?'
He said, 'Well let's talk sixteenths, how about
I have nine-sixteenths and you have seven?'
'Does that add up to the whole pizza?' I said.
'Yes, it does,' he said.
'Well then that sounds a bit more like the way
me and you eat pizza,' I said, 'yes, you probably
eat one sixteenth more than I do.'
'Two,' he said.
'Two what?' I said.
'Two sixteenths,' he said, 'which is the same as
one eighth.'
'Is it?' I said, 'why have you gone back to eighths?'
'Because that's how you do the divvying up,' he
said.
'Fair enough,' I said, 'so let's carve it up.'
I went over to the drawer and looked for the big

knife we use to cut up pizzas and it took me a
moment or two because it had got caught under one
of those strainer spoons you can buy in France.
When I came back, he was breaking chunks off the
pizza and eating them.
'Have you divvied it up into sixteenths?' I said.
'No,' he said, 'I was getting hungry so I've started
already.'
I looked at him.
'Great, you've got the pizza knife,' he said, 'do you
want to divvy it up into sixteenths, or shall I?'
I said, 'Hang on a mo. If you've started on it already,
doesn't that affect the way the divvying up works? I
mean... I mean... '
'No, he said, 'it's just the same.'

Pizza 2

I ordered a pizza the other night – Margherita with extra olives – and about twenty minutes later the pizza guy came over. He took it out of his carrier, and handed it over. I said, thanks.

He said, 'Do you want that?'

I said, 'Yes.'

He said, 'Right.'

I said, 'That's why I ordered it.'

He said, 'I thought so.'

I started to shut the door and he said, 'Any chance of giving me some?'

He said, 'If you don't want to give me some, I could buy some off you.'

I said, 'How much?'

He said, 'How about a quid for a quarter?'

I said, 'A quid! The whole pizza has cost me nearly a tenner.'

He said, 'Well, what if you take the olives off, that would make it less... you know...? '

I said, 'How about you have a bit less than a quarter and, as you say, no olives?'

He said, 'Quid, yes?'

I said, 'OK.'

I opened up the box and it was a Margherita but there were no extra olives on it.

I said, 'Looks like we can't do the olive deal.'

He said, 'The bit you were going to sell me was going to have no olives on it anyway.'

I said, 'No, no, that doesn't work. Taking olives off would have made it worth less. And anyway, I would have got extra-extra olives on the rest of my pizza.'

So he said, 'I've got an extra marshmallow in here. I could throw that in as part of the deal.'

I said, 'I'm allergic.'

He said, 'Allergic? How do you know you're

allergic to marshmallow.'

I said, 'Once when I was a kid, I ate a pack of marshmallows and got spots all over my hands.'

He said, 'You can't be sure it was the marshmallows. What else did you eat that day?'

I said, 'Probably some bread and butter. Maybe an egg. Rhubarb. I liked rhubarb.'

He said, 'Me too. I really liked rhubarb. It's funny you don't see it in the shops much.'

I said, 'No, and they say that if cows eat rhubarb leaves they die.'

He said, 'Wow. I wonder how many cows died eating rhubarb leaves.'

I said, 'No way of saying.'

He said, 'Yes, and you know how they say that you can find out anything and everything on the internet but I bet that's one fact you couldn't find.'

I said, 'Right.'

He said, 'Sorry about the olives, by the way, it's not me who does the extra olives.'

I said, 'Who does the olives?'

He said, 'Samantha, but it's her last day. She's moving to Leeds.'

I said, 'Right.'

And then he went.

Bus

I was on a bus when two people sitting behind me
started to talk to me. I said I lived nearby. They said
they did too. I said that I had lived here when I was
young. They said they hadn't lived here long. They
had met while they were doing a play. I asked them
if they were actors. Oh no, they weren't actors. They
were just in a play. Well, said one to the other, you
were in the play and I was the prompt.
'Really?' I said, 'did you do prompting every night
when the play was on?'
'Oh yes,' he said.
Then the other one said, 'And then we were in another
play and he had a part and it was me who did the
prompting.'
'Did you ever have to actually prompt?' I said.
'Yes,' she said, 'he forgot a line to do with the
radioactivity of a toaster.'
'And one night you forgot something too,' he replied.
'I don't think so,' she said back.
'Yes, the thing with the man next door who used to
do weightlifting.'
'No, when you prompted, you dived in before I said it.
I was trying to do a new pause.'
'I don't think you'd have got to the right words.'
'I would have. I know I would have. I know what I was
thinking. You don't.'
'I think you think you know what you're thinking – which
is a different matter.'
'There are times when I would like to have a prompt,'
I said.
It was that moment in the day in winter when the lights
of the shops start to be brighter than the light outside.

Euston

I was at Euston Station. An elderly woman came
up to me and started talking to me. She asked me
if she could ask me some questions.
She showed me a picture of herself in a polythene
see-through bag. I didn't look very closely at it but
I thought I saw the word 'Marketing'. My train was
delayed so I said, OK. She said that it was to improve
the service. I said, OK and she rummaged around in
her bag and took out a clip board. On the clip board
there was a list of questions.
She said, 'Are you travelling today?'
'Yes,' I said.
'Are you travelling for business, leisure or family
reasons?'
I said, 'Family reasons.'
She said, 'Do you ride a horse?'
I said, 'No.'
She said, 'When a piece of bread is smaller than
the slot in the toaster, then, assuming you turn off
the toaster for health and safety reasons, do you
a) stick a knife in the bread and hook it out?
b) pick up the toaster, turn it over and shake it out?
c) leave it in there?'
I said, 'b). I turn the toaster over.'
She said, 'Do you travel First Class or Second Class?'
I said, 'Usually Second Class, but at the weekends I might
upgrade.'
She said, 'Do you think the world political situation
would be improved if a) the Roman Empire came back b)
people stopped eating processed meat, c) politicians drank
more water?'
I said, 'I don't think any of those. Can I say none?'
She said, 'I'm the one asking the questions.'
I said, 'I know.'
She said, 'I'll take that as a).'

I said, 'The Roman Empire one?'

She said, 'Yes.'

I said, 'The Romans didn't have trains.'

She said, 'If they did, they would have made them run on time.'

I said, 'Except towards the end. You know, when they were leaving here and going back to Rome. The trains wouldn't have been on time then.'

She said, 'I've made a note of that.'

I said, 'Thanks.'

She said, 'On a scale of ten do you think the following would improve the service: "Giving customers flat-pack self-assembly furniture to construct on their journeys?" 10 for definitely, zero for not at all.'

'Nine,' I said.

'On a scale of ten, do you think customers should be supplied with the magazine, *Dairy Cow News*?'

I said, 'Nine.'

She said, 'Why?'

I said, 'Because when I was about ten years old I developed a fascination with dairy cows. I could tell the difference between a Dairy Shorthorn and an Ayrshire. I think having a free copy of *Dairy Cow News* would be of great interest.'

She said, 'The survey is complete. We give all the people we interview a small gift. You have a choice. Would you like a pen, a notebook, a tomato, a holiday in Florida or a baby?'

I said, 'I'll take the tomato.'

Prince Otto

Prince Otto acquired so much personal wealth
that he started to wonder if he had reached a
point where there really was no need for him to
do anything. His mind turned to his own body.
Surely things that took effort could and should be
done by someone else. He commissioned his
scientists to investigate the possibility of inventing
a machine that would get rid of his bodily waste
without him having to make any effort at all. Various
suggestions were made, some of which are familiar
to us today as ways of dealing with medical situations,
involving bags and tubes and the like, but Prince Otto
felt that none of these were convenient enough and,
what's more, would interfere with his pleasures. He
simply wanted someone or something to accompany
him to the usual private place and do the work for him.
Then, as he walked in his grounds, he noticed one
of his gardeners, pausing a moment in his work.
That's it, he thought to himself. Everything in life
has its opposite. There is work. And there is not-work.
All I need to do is not-work. He felt a great burden
lifted from him. The years of scientific effort and
experiment had only brought him irritation, and
on occasions, some unpleasant sensations. He
went on eating and drinking as usual. Though he
had acquired fabulous wealth he wasn't a prodigious
eater or drinker. At first, he enjoyed the feeling of
entering his private place, knowing full well that he
would be making no effort whatsoever. As far as
liquid waste was concerned, he was pleased to see
that apart from the matter of ensuring that his clothing
wasn't an obstacle, he could indeed make no effort
at all. He invented – or thought that he invented – the
'waterfall reverie' – as a means of bringing on the
process. Solid matter was, well, another matter. He

would enter the private place, perceiving that the
need was there. Resolutely, he would announce to
himself that on no account would he, Prince Otto,
make any effort whatsoever, only for him then
to find that nothing happened. He tried alternative
reveries: quarrying, fruit-picking, tipping, spending...
none of them worked. As the days went by he found
that he became sluggish and sweated more than usual.
It wasn't as though, prior to this vow, he had made much
effort anyway. It had only involved a moment of holding
the breath, a little contraction of the lower abdomen
perhaps, but nothing more. But his promise to himself
had to be kept. He would not go back on his word, even
if all it involved were such slight quantities of energy.
Needless to say, this was a matter that could not be kept
secret. As a result of his obsession, he found that he
could not proceed without telling anyone, but who could
he trust with the secret? Only his faithful hunting dog, also
called Prince Otto. So, deep in a glade in the palace park,
Prince Otto told Prince Otto the full story. No one knows
exactly how or why anyone else did get to know this story
but sure enough, the word went round:
Prince Otto (the prince, not the dog) was refusing to
make the customary effort. The effect this had on the
populace of the principality was remarkable. We might have
expected that the natural concern of the people and the
respect that they usually paid their ruler would have
produced advice, regret, compassion. Strangely on this
occasion, the first response seems to have been mostly
laughter and mockery. The second response, however, was
in its own way shocking. It was what a scientist would
call 'sympathetic action'. This is where action in one organism
or part of an organism results in similar action in another
organism or part. To put it briefly, most people in the
principality, interpreted the Prince's woes as a cue to say to
themselves, how Prince Otto behaves, so will we.
Fortunately, the people did not feel that this applied to bodily
processes, as they could see the painful consequences of so
doing. Rather, they applied it to their daily work. The outcome

of this was that Prince Otto not only suffered great physical pain, he started to experience privations in all parts of his life. Cows weren't milked, clothes weren't made, fruit wasn't picked, weapons weren't made, coaches and carts not driven. The situation could not last. There was a contest between two forces: inward and outward. Would the deprivation of everything that supplied Prince Otto with his needs – food, drink, clothing, heat – end his life; or would the amassing of his waste result in a crisis of another kind? Unfortunately, I have to close the curtains on this episode, as the information as to what happened next is not available. All that is known is that the small principality was no longer ruled by a prince and new arrangements were made for the production and distribution of goods and services. The gardener who paused for a moment in his work became a local hero. Prince Otto the dog died after many years entertaining children. You can see him in a glass case in the Palace, which is now a study centre.

Not an exit

I saw a sign: 'Not an exit'. It was on a door.
I thought that that would be a very useful
sign to have. I would put it on our fireplace
so that the cats would know not to go up
the chimney. I would put it on the fridge to
stop my children trying to leave home that
way. I would put it on the toilet bowl to stop
the goldfish from trying to find freedom through
there.

Running away

I was in the High Street, late. Just the
street lights. The department store
that isn't there anymore was up ahead.
One of the doors opened. Someone
came out. And then someone else.
They were naked. And smooth.
Then another one. And another. All
of them naked and smooth. Soon there
were ten or eleven of them. None of
them had hair. Or shoes. And they
weren't walking. Or running. More like...
sliding. Their arms didn't bend. Or their
legs. The street lights shone on their
backs. Their faces didn't move. They
didn't speak. They had no eyes.

Rabbit

I was on a children's TV programme for a short
interview. In the studio with me was a puppet.
The puppet was a rabbit. The presenter, who was
not a rabbit, asked me, 'Is Paris in France?'
I said, 'Yes.'
The rabbit said, 'Great.'
I left.
Three years later I was in a bus queue. A
man joined the queue.
He said, 'Hi.'
I said, 'Hi.'
He said, 'No?'
I said, 'I don't follow you.'
He said, 'Do you remember me?'
I said, 'I'm really sorry, I don't. I'm no good with
faces. Then when I remember faces I can never
remember the name.'
He said, 'It's Gerry. We met doing a kids' TV show.'
'Really?' I said.
'Yeah,' he said, 'I'm a puppeteer.'
'What was the show?' I said.
'You really don't remember, do you?'
'No, I don't,' I said, 'I'm really sorry.'
'*Headliners*', he said, 'with Floppy.'
'Ah, yes, *Headliners*, yes. And Floppy. The rabbit.'
'That's it,' he said and he nodded.
'You were Floppy?' I said.
'That's the one,' he said.
'The thing is,' I said, 'I don't actually remember that
we met, did we?'
'You just said we did – *Headliners* with Floppy. You
remembered.'
'Yes, but... I mean... I remember the...'
I didn't finish what I was saying.
'You remember Floppy,' he said.
'Yes,' I said, 'yes.'
He didn't say anything else. Neither did I.

Email

My email account has its own search engine.
Any word in any email can be found. This
week I searched for an email I sent about my
children's first words. The email firm said,
'Sorry, try again later.' Later the email firm
said, 'Sorry, try again later.' The email is
there but I can't get at it. I can't find it or
read it. Fifty years ago I was in hospital. They
tell me I was knocked down. They say, I lay
in a ditch talking, they put me on a table and
waited for the x-ray people to arrive. They
tell me I had my eyes open. They say, I was
talking. I try to remember this. It never comes
up. I don't know where it is.

Washing machine

I went to a washing machine re-fit place. Stacks
of washing machines. It was like washing-machine
castle-walls in there. There was a room at the back.
I walked through to it. On one of the machines it
had a bright pink star. On the star it said, 'De-shrinker
fitted'. I went over to the guy and said, 'Excuse me, it
says on one of your machines it's fitted with a
de-shrinker. What's a de-shrinker?'
'If you got something that shrunk, it de-shrinks it.'
'Takes it back to normal size?'
'Yup,' he said.
'How does it do that?' I said.
'I don't fit them,' he said, 'I'm the muscle.'
'Is it more expensive because it's got the de-
shrinker on board?' I said.
'I'll have a look,' he said.
He opened a fat book, ran down a list with his
thumb-nail.
'Yep, you pay extra for the de-shrinker.'
'Thanks,' I said, 'but I'll take one without.'
'Please yourself,' he said, 'but you don't want to
be the kind of guy who turns some tasty sweater
into a doll top and then comes running in here
giving me a hard time because you didn't buy the
one with the de-shrinker.'
'It's OK,' I said, 'I'll take one without.'
'You're not the type who takes risks, are you?' he said.
'No,' I said, 'there are pizzas I've never tried.'
'We don't do pizzas,' he said.
'You do washing machines,' I said.
'You got it,' he said.

Ticket

I once had a job at a cinema and I had to check
people's tickets. I was standing at the barrier one
Sunday and people were coming through all the
time with their tickets when a woman came up
with a piece of paper and handed it to me. I could
see straightaway that it wasn't a ticket. The tickets
were all on white pieces of paper and her bit of
paper was light green.

I said, 'I'm sorry, but this isn't a ticket.'

She said, 'I don't think you've looked at it.'

I said, 'I don't need to look at it, it's green.'

'Look at it,' she said.

'OK, I'll look at it,' I said.

It was folded over. I opened it up. On it was
written, "This could be a ticket".

I said, 'This isn't a ticket.'

She said, 'Read it.'

I said, 'I have read it.'

'No, read it out loud,' she said.

I read it out loud: "This could be a ticket."

"There you are," she said.

'No it isn't, "there you are." All it says, is "This
could be a ticket". It doesn't say that it is a ticket.'

'That's because that would be a lie. obviously,'
she said.

'Right,' I said, 'It isn't a ticket. Look there are
people waiting to come in,'

'No, no,' she said, 'the point is, it could be a
ticket.'

I said, 'Yes, yes, it could be, but it isn't.'

'But what it says there is that it's possible.
It's not impossible. There is a chance that it
could be.'

'I'm supposed to let you in, on the
off-chance that this is a ticket?' I said.

'Well,' she said, 'you don't want to be in the situation where it really was a ticket and you didn't let me in. You'd be in all sorts of trouble. Lawyers, police, stories in the papers.'
I looked at her. I looked round to see if my manager was there. She wasn't.
I said, 'OK, go in.'

Parrot

We were at the zoo when I heard a parrot
say, 'I could have been Prime Minister.'
I told the others to carry on to the Reptile
Room and I went up to the parrot and said,
'When was this?'
The parrot said, '1957.'
'Which party?'
'I can't say,' it said.
'Did you have a lot of support?' I said.
'Oh yes.'
'So it didn't turn out good for you?'
'Not sure I had the charisma,' it said.
'Really? You seem very lively.'
'That's very kind but it's not what people
said at the time,' it said.
'How about policies?' I said, 'did people
think you had good policies?'
'Oh, yes.'
'Can you tell me any of them?'
'I'm really sorry, no I can't.'
'Shame,' I said, 'I would have liked that.'
'Ah, well, you'll have to just take it
from me that they sounded really good at
the time.'
'Yes,' I said, 'shame all the same.'
'Well,' it said, sounding a bit irritated, 'you
can't expect me to remember everything.
Some of us can only remember, "Who's
a pretty boy?"'
'And there's one I knew who used to say
"Alright, Mark?," I said.
'I don't know that one,' it said.

Sculptor

One of the greatest sculptors of the fourteenth
century was an Italian. Up until recently, that's all
we knew about him apart from the fact that he
probably lived in or near Florence and that his
personal life was a matter of gossip and concern.
There are passing third hand comments in city records
referring to 'misdeeds' and to a talented sculptor
'of the shadows'. As no misdeeds can be connected
to the sculptures, and as 'of the shadows' could mean
almost anything, no one has taken these comments
particularly seriously. To make matters more
'of the shadows', if you like, it's never been
fully possible to match a name with a particular
set of statues. Art historians are able to attribute
a cluster of works to one sculptor whom they have
always called 'Alessandro' due to the fact that the
monogram 'Ao' has been found engraved on the sole of
the foot of one of statues. But as others have
pointed out, the 'Ao' could just as easily refer to the
owner or even the carrier who would have taken
the statue by cart to an owner. Even so, the statues
themselves have, in recent years, been recognised
as some of the most remarkable work from this
early period of the renaissance. There is every
possibility that Michelangelo would have laid eyes
on them and their realism could easily have
awakened his sense of how raw rock could come
to express the essence of what it is to be human.
The pathos expressed in Ao's 'Narcissus' has been
described as the very first post-classical sculpture
to express 'pain in stone'.

Now, very recently, a drama – a crisis even – has
taken place in the world of renaissance art criticism.
Word is coming out of Italy which suggests a scandal

of great significance: rumours and rumours of
rumours which start to flesh out why this phrase
'of the shadows' may have come down to us in the 21st
century attached to 'Alessandro'. It would appear
that the Narcissus was being moved so that
it could be exhibited in an exhibition to celebrate
the 700th anniversary of the patronage of the
de Brunelli family. It seems that the pulley
system being used was faulty, ('faulty' perhaps,
by way of 'payback' for non-payment of hiring fees,
though there was a long-standing dispute between
the family of the art removal people and the 'owner'
of the statue – the ownership of the statue is itself
disputed owing to a sale that was not fully paid for
(allegedly) in the 1880s.) The substantive matter
though is that the statue fell to the ground when
the pulley's retention ratchet failed to function.
As a result the statue broke.

At first glance, what was remarkable, so it's
said, is that it cracked open along a line, like
an easter egg can sometimes be cracked neatly
in half. The immediate thought of those who
were there, was that 'Alessandro' had experimented
with some kind of double bas-relief process that had
never been seen before. However, in a matter of
moments, it became clear that something of much
greater significance had taken place. Within the statue,
in its heart, if you like, was a skeleton.

At present, the matter is under investigation.
I have no further information as to the sex of
the person. The possibility of a female skeleton
inside the body of Narcissus invites a variety of
interpretations. Narcissus engulfing Echo?
Forensic archaeologists should be able to
determine the age of the person, and
indeed their status and by analysis of the bones
a good deal to do with their diet, the nature of

the water that he or she drunk and from that, the probable whereabouts of their dwelling-place. To date, we do not know if any other of the statues attributed to 'Alessandro' have been investigated. Part of the problem is the question of disputed ownership. The matter is further complicated by a local Italian law concerning what is known as the 'right of discourse'. Even if the ownership can be determined, the 'right of discourse' is in dispute. In other words, until this is sorted, no one has the right to publish any information concerning any investigation taking place from the date that the 'right of discourse' injunction was served. The information in this article is in the public domain but anything else is proscribed. If anyone does publish any material deriving from an investigation post the time of the injunction, the ultimate victor in that dispute will have total right to pursue the publisher of that information for full recompense. Others have spoken of the value of Narcissus – 'value' in all senses of the word. Clearly, what is taking place all over the art world is a 're-evaluation'.

Imagine, therefore, a situation in which a media organisation like NBC or *Time Life* published a story in which it emerged that the skeleton inside the statue was of modern origin and was linked to a well-known politician – and of course this is totally hypothetical on my part – then the damages would be enormous. One could imagine that the consequence could even bankrupt a media conglomerate anywhere in the world.

Tea

They've opened up a new cafe round our way
so I thought I'd give it a try. You go up to the
counter to choose and the menu is high up
on the wall. I saw 'Homemade Tomato'.
I said, 'I'll have the Homemade Tomato, please.'
'Anything else?' the man said.
'I'll have a cup of tea with that, please.'
'Usual?' he said.
'I haven't been in this cafe before,' I said.
'I know you haven't,' he said, 'I meant do you
want the tea you usually drink.'
'Yes please,' I said.
'And what kind of tea is that?' he said, 'I don't
know what kind of tea that is.'
I said, 'I'll have English breakfast,'
'I've got a breakfast tea here,' he said, 'but it
doesn't say that it's English.'
'I'm not bothered about the English,' I said.
'Oh aren't you?' he said, 'It's all got a bit political,
hasn't it?'
'I tell you what, I said, can I have a coffee? Black
Americano.'
He winked. I winked back. I wasn't sure why I
winked. It felt like the right thing to do at the time.
I sat down.
A few minutes later he came to my table. He had
the coffee and a plate with a tomato on it. He
turned and went back to behind the counter. I
drank some coffee and started on the tomato. He
hadn't brought a knife and fork, so I reckoned that
the best way to eat it was like you eat an apple.
Pick it up and bite into it. I took pretty small bites
because I'd been caught out like that before. You
take a big bite into a tomato and you end up with
tomato all over yourself. To tell the truth I'm not

mad keen on tomato by itself. I really like it with bread. Or cut in half and grilled with toast. Or chopped up with cucumber and Greek parsley and a bit olive oil and lemon juice. He didn't have that on the menu.

Streamlining

I noticed that there have been some improvements
at the station I use: streamlining of services.
A couple of years ago they figured out that we don't
need indicator boards which tell you of every single
station the trains go to. All they needed to do was
put up the names of the last station on the line. This
meant that getting a train became an interesting kind
of guesswork. Would the train to Bigtown stop at
Littletown? Or would the train to Redtown be the
right one for Littletown? It was great. You could stand
on the wrong platform at the right time. Or the right
platform at the wrong time. Or the wrong platform at
the wrong time.

Then, they figured out that the indicator board thing
was a luxury. So they did away with them. Now, you
arrive at the station and guess which train might be
yours. Sometimes, you can wait on one platform, a
train comes in on another. You think it might be yours.
You dash along your platform, down the stairs, along
a tunnel, up some stairs on to the other platform... and
the train is leaving. You dash back down the stairs, along
the tunnel, up the stairs, back to the platform you were
on in the first place.

Some people get up in the morning and think, I wonder
where I'll go today? They head to the station and just get
on any train that looks like a train they might want to get
on.

Use the stairs

It said, 'Please use the stairs', so everyone turned right at the end of the platform. Someone with a buggy hesitated and there was a blockage behind it. Someone grabbed the front and the flow carried on. At the bottom of the steps there was a tunnel. It turned sharply. We followed it round. There must have been hundreds of us. Someone was whistling. A man near me was doing that sniff-cough thing: sniffing hard, which made him cough. We weren't really walking. Shuffling, more like. Then the tunnel turned again. More steps going down. We glanced at each other. Just because the escalators weren't working, surely we didn't need to be going quite so far down? At the end of these steps there was another tunnel. It seemed temporary: no advertisements on the wall. And no tiles either. Just raw cement. Then the lights flickered and dimmed. That set off some shouting. A child up ahead started to scream. A few people were talking, asking each other if they knew this part of the station. Someone near me said that it was the 'Transit Route' for the maintenance crew and we would come out by the post office. Someone way back shouted that they were sorry the lights had failed, asked us to be patient and it would be sorted as soon as possible. We carried on shuffling, though much more slowly. The floor was untiled too. More like gravel. After a spell of this, it became less dark, and the tunnel opened out into a chamber, a kind of hall. Now there were one or two station staff, holding out their arms at full stretch sideways, as if they were making a passageway. And nodding. I thought, what's with the nodding? One of them was saying, 'This way.' There was no other way. As people filed into the hall behind me, another station person started making an announcement on a megaphone: '...thanks very much for your patience... not an emergency... precautions... security... held here for a short while...'

Then she said that it would greatly help if we could separate into two groups, those who travelled regularly on the transport system and those who were new to it. People started filtering right and left and I heard an argument near me when someone said that a child couldn't be someone who had 'travelled regularly on the transport system'. The father – if that's who it was – started shouting, 'What do you want me to do with him? He's five years old. Send him over there on his own?' And he got the reply, 'Well that's what they're asking.' One or two people couldn't understand what was going on and were trying to find out more. So people were pointing over to the side of the hall for people who 'don't travel regularly on the transport system'. I had a sense that those of us who do 'travel regularly on the transport system' were being let down another tunnel and we shuffled off down it and there were more staff with their arms out, nodding. The people who 'didn't travel regularly on the transport system' stayed behind in the hall. At the other end of our tunnel there were some steps up to the street but it wasn't by the post office. It was nowhere near the post office.

Waking up

He found a way of waking himself up.
As he was going to sleep he kept
saying to himself, 'Wake up! Wake up!'
He dozed off with these words in his
mind, over and over again, 'Wake up!
Wake up! Wake up!'

At around 7 in the morning he found
himself dreaming that he was asleep
in the back of a car and someone
was outside the car, shouting,
'Wake up! Wake up! Wake up!'
In his dream, he woke up and
because he knew he was in his
dream he wondered if that meant
he was still asleep.
Still in his dream, he realised
who it was who was shouting,
'Wake up! Wake up! Wake up!'
It was him. The person outside the
car was him.

Still in his dream he stared at
himself. The 'him' that was shouting
'Wake up!' stared at the 'him' who
had woken up. 'You're still asleep!'
he shouted. 'You think you've woken
up but that's in the dream. In fact
you're asleep.'
'Then who are you?' the sleeping
him said.
'I'm the you, who is waking you up,'
he said.
'But you're in the dream, so you're
asleep as well, aren't you?' he said.

'Yes,' said the him that was waking
him up.
'So how will you wake up?' he asked.
'I don't know,' he said, 'all I know
is that I have to wake you up.'
'But how can you wake me up
if you're asleep?'

That morning, he woke up later
than he had ever woken up before.

Moving

I once had to hire a van to move some of my
stuff. I got it from one of those guys who loan
out vans from an arch under the railway. He
said that I didn't need to check over the scratches
because he didn't charge for that anyway. He
just checked out that all the insurance was in
place and I went off. When I got to my place,
I went upstairs to get the first boxes, came
down to the street, opened up the back door
and a boy jumped out. He must have been
waiting for someone to unlock the door and
he was off up the street, running faster than
I could catch him. I wasn't going to call the police.
He hadn't done me any harm. As far as I could
see, he hadn't done any harm to the van. I had to
clean it up, if you get me. But he had used a bag,
so it wasn't too bad. There were some crumbs.
And some plum stones. And some caraway
seeds. They smell a bit like aniseed. When I
was a kid, we used to have caraway seed
bread. It was like my parents liked to remember
what their parents ate, and they had eaten it
to remember the place they came from. Some
of my friends said that I smelled of it.

Wasp

I was swatting a wasp with my
fly swat when I heard it say,
'Cut that out, you're swatting
the wrong guy, I'm on your side.
I'm an undercover wasp fighting
for you.'
I said, 'I'm not fighting anyone.'
He said, 'Oh yes you are, look
at that swat. One swipe through
the air and BLAM! and I'm
done for. It may not look like
war to you, but it sure looks
like that to us.'
'Us?' I said, 'who are you talking
about with this "us"? A moment ago,
you were on my side. Now it's "us".
So you're not on my side, are you?'
'Yes I am,' he said, 'but I'm still
a wasp. I think like a wasp, I
do wasp stuff.'
'I don't get this,' I said, 'I'm just
trying to stop you stinging me.'
'What's stinging got to do with it?'
he said, 'what is it with you people
on and on about stinging...?
Sting, sting, sting.'
'That's because you sting,' I said.
'But it's not all we do,' he said,
'we're not just stingers. We're
wasps.'
'Yes, yes,' I said, 'but you do sting,
and I've discovered
this way to stop you stinging:
it is what you said it was: swipe,
BLAM! That stops the stinging.'

'Yes, yes, I know,' he said,
'but you're not listening to me:
I'm as much against stinging as you.'

Just then, another wasp turned up.
'C'mon, let's go,' he said.
'Sure,' said my wasp, 'this guy
isn't worth the hit.'
'What do you mean, "not
worth the hit"?' I said, 'what's
the matter with me?'
They flew off.

The wasp lady

I was playing by a river in France when
an old lady came past and the boy I was
with said that was the Wasp Lady. I asked
him why she was called the Wasp Lady
and he said that she gets rid of wasps'
nests. I asked him how she does that. He
said that she had a special way. 'What
sort of special way?' I said. He laughed
and said that he wasn't supposed to say.
I said, 'Why aren't you supposed to say?'
He said that the people in the village
didn't want children to go about saying it.
I said, 'How does she do it? How does
she get rid of wasps' nests?' He said that
she stands by the wasps' nest and sings.
'That's it?' I said. 'Yes,' he said. 'Then
what happens?' I said. He then said it
wasn't really singing. It was more like a
single note. She stands by the nest
trying to sing this note. It's not like any
singing you ever hear, he said. 'Like
what?' I said and he just laughed. We
went on mucking about in the river and
I said, 'What does this singing thing do?'
He said that if she gets it right, people
say that it makes the wasps eat the queen.
I said, 'That wouldn't get rid of the nest.'
He said that it would. If the queen goes,
all the rest die off after a few days. If
there are no new eggs, there are no new
wasps, that's the end of the nest. 'Do they
sting the queen?' I said. 'I don't know,' he
said, 'I think they just eat her. They hear
the singing and start to eat her.'

Painting

We turned up in the yard because there
was an ad in the paper. There was a man
there who asked us if we had ever done any
painting before. I said yes. He sent me to
the top of a ladder and on to a plank. It was
high up, under the roof. There was no ceiling.
I had to paint what was the underside of the
roof. There were three of us up there. It was an
empty factory, or a hangar. Our plank was about
seven feet under the roof so we had to paint
above our heads. There were no safety rails.
The man said it was best not to look down.

It was a hot day, the sun shining on to the roof
outside. It wasn't just that it was hot doing painting.
The roof was hot. The man said we were toshers.
Just put it on. And get it done. As the paint went on,
the heat made it fume. I could feel it spread out
under my face, into the spaces behind my eyes. It
made me smile. Thick cream paint.

I looked across to the other guys. They were
toshing. I smiled. They smiled. One of them laughed.
Don't look down, he said. I'm not sure he said
it to me. He may have said it to the other guy. I nodded.
He nodded. There was a day at the beach. The
sand was a million fragments of glass, each
pointing towards my eyes. There was a link between
my eyes and being sick. You could look at
the brightness for so long that it flowed into your
stomach. Light waves making sick waves.
There was a presentation day once and
everyone was told to go on to the platform, shake
hands and get off the platform as quickly as
possible but this boy Jeff, got up there and waved.

He waved to his mates and they all cheered. And
that had been wrong. Jeff was wrong. He had done
a wrong thing. Jeff was wrong to have done that.
The paint was white. The smile was more like a grin
now. Like I had to pull my lips back to make room
for the fumes in my face.

The roof moved. The paint was white. The waves
reached my legs. Milk into a bucket from the cow.
Thick with bubbles. You could paint with milk.
Warm milk with cream. And it's cream that makes
butter. Shaking it up till it gets thicker. It's the
shaking that makes it thick.

I had to kneel down. I knelt down. I looked
across to the other guys. One of them was standing.
He had stopped painting. He was standing. I said,
'Whooo.' He said, 'Yeahh.' I said, 'I'm kneeling.' Then
he knelt down too. I said, 'I'm going to lie down
now. I'm going to lie down.' I lay down on the plank.
He lay down on the plank too. I looked at the other
guy. He was pressing on. 'He's good,' I said.
He said, 'Don't shut your eyes.' I shut my eyes.

Groundsheet

If you put a tent up on long grass and you leave the tent with its groundsheet down on the grass for about three weeks, the grass starts to rot. When you take up the groundsheet, you find the grass has gone yellow and smells. Worms seem to like it and sometimes you find clusters of them wiggling about together. One holiday we were on the Welsh borders and our tents were up for four weeks. We took them down when it was time to go home and there was a cluster of worms just where I had been lying. I went over and had a look at them. As I walked round them, I could see that they had clustered together in the shape of the bus routes near where we lived. I called my friend over and said, 'Here look at this, it's the bus map.' He said, 'Oh yeah.' He looked at it closely and then he noticed something: 'There's no 43. The 43 is missing.' He was right. 'The map would be no good without the 43,' he said. 'The 43 is a really useful route. The 43 goes all the way down the Holloway Road.'

London Fields

Evening falls between the trees
The drumming for Ghana fills the leaves

All along the cycle path
The racers, the white dreads
The market shoppers
The tandem parents

The drumming for Ghana fills the leaves
Evening falls between the trees

And here a Plane tree
Higher than a warehouse
Thicker than a rubbish bin
Stronger than a promise
Older than a town hall

Evening falls between the trees
The drumming for Ghana fills the leaves

The train for Liverpool street
Groans over the bridge
Children climb the spider's web
If you don't come home
You'll have no sweets for a week

Evening falls between the trees
The drumming for Ghana fills the leaves

And here a Plane tree
higher than a warehouse
Thicker than a rubbish bin
Stronger than a promise
Older than a town hall

The wicket falls
High fives all round
Conkers shining in their nests
Mr Softee pulls away
She makes love to her mobile
So happy he's called

Evening falls between the trees
The drumming for Ghana fills the leaves

Here a plane tree
Higher than a warehouse
Thicker than a rubbish bin
Stronger than a promise
Older than a Town hall.

Traffic

I got caught in some traffic the other day. A car had stopped up ahead. I thought that it had broken down. People started getting out of their cars and beeping their horns. Someone walking on the pavement alongside me was pointing. I got out and walked up the street. There was a car with no driver in it, in the middle of a single lane. The door was open and a man was standing in front of a car looking down at the road. He was shouting. As I got nearer, I could see that he was staring at the sign on the surface of the road where it said SLOW and he was shouting, 'I'm not, I'm not!'

Bear Grylls

This poem is going to test whether you can survive.
It's going to test whether you have the character
to cope with anything that this poem might
throw at you.
This poem is unforgiving and indifferent.
It doesn't care if you live or die.
It's just you and the poem.

After this first part of the poem,
I'm going to have to make a choice.
I can tell already that some of you aren't physically
or mentally strong enough
to stick with the whole poem.
You're going to drop out.

The next part is going to be an even bigger test.
In and amongst the words there might be a
metaphor or some alliteration.
You're going to have to ask yourself
what single thing is going to get me through.
You might have to grab a word,
squeeze it – even eat it –
because this poem is like a forest that you've got to
get through.
You have to use whatever it takes,
even if it means eating the person next to you.
That's what life is like.
Sometimes you just have to eat people.

Hah!
I told you to look out for metaphors and alliteration
but that bit about the forest was a simile.
I said this poem is LIKE a forest.
Some of you missed that.
People who miss things, die.

Just because I say, look out for one thing
it doesn't mean that something else won't be
lurking in there.
It can happen in a split second.
It can be something you hadn't reckoned
with.
Hah!
That was a hidden rhyme.
And some of you ignored it
but it went into your head anyway
and that's the difference between life and death.

In a moment, I'm going to have to choose
which one of you has got what it takes
to come with me on the rest of this poem.

It has to be someone who I think is good enough,
someone, who, if pushed, would be prepared
to eat their own face if it meant they could get
to the end of a poem.

Now, for the time being, go off to your tent
there's another whole day of poems tomorrow,
and one of you is going to die of poetry.

Shirts

I had two light blue shirts.
They were identical. Exactly the same.
Just two of them.
I didn't buy them.
They were given to me by a TV company.
Wear the shirts, they said, when the one you've
been wearing is dirty, take it off, put on the other one,
no one will notice the difference, we'll wash the first one
and when the second one is dirty, you can put the first one
on again.
At the end of the series, they gave me the shirts.
I've had them ever since.
I think that's 6 years I've had them. Two light blue shirts.
I wear them really often.

The other morning, very early, I went downstairs,
switched on the light and next to the washing machine
there were my two light blue shirts.
And another one. Exactly the same as the other two.
There were three light blue shirts. Identical.
Hanging from a water-pipe next to the boiler.
Three shirts.

Guide to the sixties

for journalists who want to hear what they want to hear
doing 50th anniversary articles

In the sixties we all went to Woodstock
we all protested
and we all grew beards,
apart from the women.
The sixties were great but most people
were shot or died from an overdose.
In the sixties we did songs, drugs and
aubergines.
There didn't used to be aubergines.
Then there were loads of them.
The sixties ended class.
The Beatles showed that there was no
more working class,
middle class and upper class.
There were just vibes.
Good vibes and bad vibes.
People went on TV and said fuck.
They said, here now is the nine o'clock
fucking news.
Women became feminists,
did loads of sex and stopped having babies.
Here's something:
no one in the sixties wore suits
now everyone from the sixties wears suits.
What does that tell you, eh?
When we look back on the sixties
we say it was great but the sixties
couldn't last into the seventies.
Apart from Bob Dylan.

An atheistical thought

The simplest and easiest way to be an atheist is to just be it and do it. If you don't want to, you don't have to argue it or try to prove it. You just do all the big things and all the small things – everything – without ever referring to any kind of supernatural force. You can have wonder, mystery, tragedy, ecstasy, love, hate, memory, foresight, wisdom, music, foolishness or whatever – and none of it needs to be hooked to a deity. If it already comes that way – attached to a god or to worship – so be it. That's how they thought it or lived it in their day, in their time. But those who did that cannot prescribe how you must think it or live it. And an atheist doesn't have to tell the believer how to think it or believe it.

Your dog

I quite like your dog
but I do not love your dog.
I do not love your dog barking
if anyone comes within a hundred yards
of your front door.
I do not love your dog sniffing my balls.
I do not love your dog.

I do not love your dog
just because it is a dog.
I do not love your dog
just because you love your dog.
I do not love playing football
right where your dog has crapped.
I do not love your dog's dog crap.
I do not love your dog.

I do not love your dog
when it tries to kill another dog.
I do not love the other dog.
I do not love your dog in the shop
where it says 'No dogs'.
I do not love your dog when it licks my face.
I do not love your dog when you say
he's only being friendly.
I quite like your dog
but I do not love your dog.

Leather

When I grow up
I'm going to live in Leatherland.
I'm going to have leather chairs
and leather tables, leather shoes,
and leather socks,
a leather fridge and leather doors,
a leather kettle and leather pictures
on leather walls.
There'll be a leather sink with leather taps
a leather bath and a leather loo.
Leather soap, leather loo paper,
and leather water.
We'll cook on a leather cooker
and eat leather chips with leather
peas, sprinkled with leather salt.
We'll have leather ice cream
and drink leather juice.
And when birthdays come
we'll have leather cake.
We'll have a leather cat
who'll eat leather Whiskas
and catch leather mice.
In the evenings we'll watch leather telly
and sleep in leather beds
and have leather dreams.

The dentist and the toe

I was at the dentist and when he had finished
I said, 'One of my toes is hurting, could you
take a look at it while I'm here?'
He said, 'Sure.'
I took off my shoes and socks and he looked
closely at the toe I was talking about.
He said, 'I can do a variety of things here, I
can drill down behind the nail and then give you
a temporary filling; I could take a mould, then
remove the toe and give you a new toe; or
I could send you to a chiropodist.'
I said, 'I like the sound of the new toe.'
So he said, 'Fine,' and got to work straightaway.
It all went well. This was a few weeks ago
and I've got the new toe. It's OK – not great
though. It's a bit inflexible because it's made
of the stuff they fill teeth with. I was talking to
someone the other day about it, and she said
that all I had probably needed to do was
cut my nails a bit more carefully.

Cocoa

Under London Bridge Station
there are arches which are let out to cafes
and food stores.
One was selling chocolates.
It said they came from a 'British Cocoa Grower'.
Why did they think I cared that the cocoa grower
was British?
Did they think I was more likely to buy their chocolates
if I knew that the person owning the cocoa plantation
was British?
Would it make me pleased to know that the person
employing the people who pick the cocoa beans
is British?
Would I eat the chocolate thinking, 'Mmm, this British-owned
cocoa-beans chocolate tastes yummy?'
Do they think that I think that British Cocoa plantation owners are
better, nicer, friendlier, fairer, more sympatico than all other
kinds of cocoa growers?

Maybe on TV soon, there will be a programme
called the Great British Cocoa-off.
I look forward to that.

A photo of a milking machine

A photo of a milking machine
won't tell you
how fast the milk is going into the tank.
It won't tell you
whether the milk going in is speeding up
or slowing down
nor whether it's going in faster or slower than
it did yesterday.
And – come to think of it:
it won't tell you whether the milk is going
from the cow into the tank
or from the tank
into the cow.

Card trick without cards

He said:
I can do card tricks without cards.
I said:
Great.
He said:
Pick a card.
I said:
OK.
He said:
Have you done it?
I said:
Yes.
He said:
Put it back in the pack.
I said:
OK.
He said:
I'm shuffling the pack.
I said:
Great.
He said:
Is it this one?
I said:
Which one?
He said:
This one.
I said:
But you haven't said which one it is.
He said:
I told you, I haven't got a pack.
I said:
Right, I get you. Yes, it is that one. You picked the right one.
He said,
I know.

Notes

Lions

Since the very early years of the Fitzwilliam Museum in Cambridge four stone lions have been positioned outside the museum, two at the north steps and two at the south steps. In 1816 Richard, VII Viscount Fitzwilliam of Merrion, bestowed his library and collection of art to the University of Cambridge as well as £100,000 to construct a building that would house them. His aim was to further 'the Increase of Learning and other great Objects of that Noble Foundation.' It was not until 1835, after a process of discussions and land acquisition, that the Syndicate overseeing the project selected an architect who would design the building. After advertising the tender in the newspapers the Syndicate selected George Basevi (1794–1845), a London-born architect, from a group of 27 architects who had sent in plans to be considered. Two years later, on the 4th November 1837, the the Vice-Chancellor, Gilbert Ainslie, laid the foundation stone of the Fitzwilliam Museum, below where the northern lions rest.

In that same year the sculptor William Grinsell Nicholl (1796-1871) became involved in the task of creating the monumental lions that overlook Trumpington Street, when he was commissioned to realise Basevi's architectural vision. Nicholl had started work that year carving decorative details of Basevi's designs for the museum, working on the Corinthian columns and the decorative aspects of the façade. Then in 1839 he sculpted the four iconic lions that guard the south and north steps to the Fitzwilliam Museum's portico entrance.

According to local folklore, when the Church of Our Lady and the English Martyrs' clock strikes midnight, the Fitzwilliam Lions rise from their plinths and make their way to drink from the gutters that run along Trumpington Street, a few metres from where they sit, sometimes walking as far as Hobson's Conduit. According to different versions, they are also said to enter the museum, passing through the walls and occasionally letting out a roar. This is the inspiration for this poem, which is located at the Fitzwilliam Museum steps.

They shall not pass

Shmatte is a Yiddish word for rag; the '*shmatte* trade' is thus the rag trade.